LUCK

THE ESSENTIAL GUIDE

THE SOCIETY FOR FORTUITOUS EVENTS

DEBORAH AARONSON AND KEVIN KWAN, TRUSTEES

Collins

An Imprint of HarperCollinsPublishers

FIRST EDITION

Design and illustrations by Lara Harris

Library of Congress Cataloging-in-Publication Data

Aaronson, Deborah.
Luck : the essential guide : the society for fortuitous events /
Deborah Aaronson and Kevin Kwan.—1st ed.
p. cm.
Includes index.
ISBN 978-0-06-149115-3
1. Fortune. I. Kwan, Kevin. II. Title.

BF1778.A27 2008
398'.41—dc22
2007046193

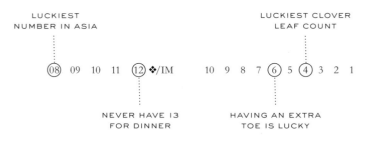

LUCKIEST
NUMBER IN ASIA

08   09   10   11   (12) ♣/IM

NEVER HAVE 13
FOR DINNER

LUCKIEST CLOVER
LEAF COUNT

10   9   8   7   (6)   5   (4)   3   2   1

HAVING AN EXTRA
TOE IS LUCKY

TABLE OF CONTENTS

LUCKY CHARMS

If you've ever found yourself wondering why
something is lucky, wonder no more. Following is a
veritable greatest hits of lucky charms—the ones
people have relied on for centuries to bring them good
fortune. In each case, we've attempted to separate
fact from superstition to explain how these charms
came to be lucky and, perhaps most importantly,
tell how you can use them. Although most of the time
the explanations make perfect sense, occasionally
the draw of an object or practice defies plausible
explanation. Sometimes a lucky charm is, well,
just a lucky charm, and either you're drinking the
Kool-Aid or holding out for a Diet Coke.

```
ABRACADABRA
BRACADABR
RACADAB
ACADA
CAD
A
```

WHY IT IS LUCKY

Long before magicians used it in vaudeville acts, the word *abracadabra* was invested with lucky powers. People in search of good fortune were advised to write out the word repeatedly, eliminating some of the letters with each repetition, in the shape of an upside-down triangle. Worn as a charm around the neck, it was believed to bring good luck and to cure any ailment the wearer might be suffering from. Eventually the belief migrated from the written word to the spoken word, and the term was used by magicians accompanied by scantily clad women before pulling a rabbit out of a hat. First mentioned by the Gnostic physician Quintus Serenus Sammonicus in the second century AD, the word may find its origins in Hebrew, some suggest; in Egyptian, others suggest. Explanations are plentiful and all seem equally probable.

HOW TO USE IT

Although wearing a charm instead of visiting a medical professional is never recommended, *abracadabra* charms are readily available and may be worn for luck. It's also possible to take a piece of paper, write the words out, fold the paper into the shape of a cross, and then wear that. Bad luck will decrease, and therefore good luck will increase, as the words grow shorter. After nine days, throw the paper over your shoulder into an eastern-flowing river.

ACORN

WHY IT IS LUCKY

Some purport that the belief in the luck of the acorn has grown out of the nut's association with the oak tree, which has been considered sacred at least as far back as the Vikings. The oak was closely identified with the god Thor, who was known to ride through the skies during thunderstorms, creating lightning by smashing his hammer. Although trees themselves are great attractors of lightning, it was believed that Thor specifically spared the oak—and its acorns—his wrath. Others believe that Druids made particular use of acorns in divining rituals and wore them as charms for good luck. Others still believe the acorn's lucky properties are related to a much simpler meaning: the triumphant acorn-turned-oak symbolizes tenacity and longevity.

HOW TO USE IT

Today it's easy to purchase an acorn charm made of silver or gold. Many people believe that carrying a real acorn in your pocket (or pocketbook) is a way to ensure good luck and a long life. An acorn (real or imitation) can also be placed on a windowsill or hung from a window shade to protect a home from undesirable meteorological events. Acorns are also thought to be useful in love divination. Place two in a bowl of water (one is you; the other, the object of your affection). If they float close together, you're headed for the altar.

BEGINNER'S LUCK

WHY IT IS LUCKY

We've all experienced winning a game we've never played before or surpassing a well-seasoned competitor our first time around at something. Although some suggest this success stems from the lack of psychological pressure the novice undergoes, we all experience a certain amount of stress when performing a task, even when expectations are low. Lacking a clear, logical explanation as to why a neophyte should excel at something never before attempted, many people simply chalk the phenomenon up to "beginner's luck." Many luck-centered beliefs relate to the significance of the beginning or first of something, whether it's a new year, a new life, a new purchase, or a new business venture. It's not a great leap from there to assume that first-timers at any task would carry with them some of the same lucky potential as these other auspicious firsts do. And lucky for him, the beginner just has to show up.

HOW TO USE IT

Make sure you take full advantage of your beginner's luck—after all, you only have it once. You can also use someone else's beginner's luck to your own advantage. If you're planning a trip to the casino or have a crucial match to play, invite a newbie friend to join you.

BLUE

WHY IT IS LUCKY

Although there's nothing lucky about having a case of the blues, the Bible singles out the color blue as significant, and it endures in both the flag of Israel and as the color most closely associated with the Virgin Mary. It also makes frequent appearances in idiomatic expressions, where "blue blood" is a sign of nobility, and someone who remains loyal is "true blue." And although many of us have only heard the phrase in reference to the children's television program *Blue's Clues*, the Blue-clue was first and foremost an eighteenth-century love-divination tool involving a clew (skein) of blue yarn, a cauldron, and the belief that the two together would help you identify your true love. In the nineteenth and early twentieth centuries, men were known to wear blue stocking supporters, children blue ribbons around their necks, and women strands of blue beads—all for luck and protection. And, of course, no bride should be without "something blue" to help bring her good fortune.

HOW TO USE IT

Even if you're not a bride, venturing into any situation wearing something blue is sure to provide luck.

BODY LANGUAGE

Even when we're not speaking, our bodies communicate a
wealth of information. Here are some lucky things to look for.

HAIR	Safeguarding a lock of your baby's hair is not only a sentimental gesture; it will also protect her from serious harm. Redheads can bring good luck to the person who rubs their hands or a pair of dice on them—just don't forget to ask permission first. A hairy person, however unappealing, is said to be lucky. It's unlucky, though, to cut your hair on Fridays or Sundays.
EYES	An eyelash that falls out may be placed on the back of your hand and blown away as you make a wish. A twitching eyelid is a sign of good luck. To meet a cross-eyed person (notably a woman) is considered lucky.
EARS	In Japan it is considered lucky to have big ears, and in China big earlobes are a sign of good fortune.
NOSE	Sneezing once or three times in a row is a bad sign, but sneezing twice is considered lucky. If you sneeze at the same time as another person, you'll both enjoy good luck. Sneezing should always be responded to with a verbal response, be it "bless you" or "gesundheit," for luck.

TEETH	A gap between your front teeth suggests you will be lucky, wealthy, and travel widely.
TONGUE	In mid-nineteenth-century England, some people were known to carry around what was called the "lucky bit," the tip of a cow's or ox's tongue, for luck.*
HANDS	It is generally considered luckier to use your right hand rather than your left, although it's lucky to meet a left-handed person on the street. Rubbing hands with a person who has just had a run of luck might allow their good fortune to rub off on you.
FINGERS	Of course, crossing your fingers is a well-documented antidote to bad luck. To have white spots on your nails is a sign of good luck. However, as with hair, it's unlucky to cut your fingernails on Fridays or Sundays.
FEET	It's always luckiest to enter a place right foot first. To be born with an extra toe is considered lucky.
HEART	Although in ancient times the liver was considered the seat of love, today wearing jewelry in the shape of a heart is believed to make you lucky in love. Besides, Tiffany's doesn't make a liver-shaped charm.

Although this has nothing to do with a human tongue, we couldn't resist including it.

LUCKY CHARMS

BUTTON

WHY IT IS LUCKY

Although many people know that four-leaf clovers and horseshoes can bring good luck, fewer know that buttons are not only harbingers of good fortune, but they can also be more predictive of career paths than the Myers-Briggs personality test. Buttons have been around since ancient times, although until buttonholes were invented in the thirteenth century they were largely ornamental. They are thought to be especially lucky when either found by accident or received as a gift, regardless of the fact that no one seems to know why this is the case.

HOW TO USE IT

Make sure when you are getting dressed that you put each button into its proper buttonhole. If you don't, bad luck will follow you all day. To prevent this, remove the piece of clothing entirely and start again. For a spousal career prediction, grab a bunch of loose buttons and recite:

> *"A doctor, a lawyer, a merchant, a chief, / A rich man,*
> *a poor man, a beggar-man, a thief"*

while counting out your buttons. Whichever job corresponds to the last button will be your future mate's profession. You can also try the British version, but you'll need a lot more buttons:

> *"Tinker, tailor, soldier, sailor, / Gentleman, apothecary, / Plowboy, thief. /*
> *Soldier brave, sailor true, / Skilled physician, Oxford blue, /*
> *Learned lawyer, squire so hale, / Dashing airman, curate pale. / Army,*
> *Navy, / Medicine, Law, / Church, nobility, / Nothing at all."*

CHIMNEY SWEEPS

WHY THEY ARE LUCKY

Running into a chimney sweep is not as common as it used to be, although it's always good luck when you do. One legend that purports to explain the luck of the sweep tells the story of a chimney sweep who saved the life of a king. Since the man's face was blackened from working in the soot, the king and his retinue had no way of knowing who he was. From that day forward, whenever the king and the members of his court encountered a sweep, they acknowledged him with a greeting or by taking off their hats—just in case he was the sweep who had saved the king's life. It followed that all people showed the same reverence to sweeps, and from this grew the idea that it was lucky to do so.

HOW TO USE THEM

If you happen to see a sweep, bow to him, greet him, or, if you have his permission, touch him or shake his hand for "sweeps' luck." To encounter a sweep on New Year's Day or on your wedding day is thought to be particularly auspicious. The luck is increased if the sweep walks a way with the bridal couple or gives the bride a kiss. It's been said that some sweeps, knowing their value on the luck market, have made more money working wedding receptions than they have cleaning chimneys.

CLOCKWISE MOTION

WHY IT IS LUCKY

Worship of the sun was fundamental to many ancient cultures, and countless myths, rituals, and festivals paid homage to the star's supremacy. As a result, emulating the sun by turning to the right (or clockwise) was believed to be a way of increasing luck or changing it for the good. Funeral-goers were supposed to approach the graveyard and wedding processions to enter the churchyard from a sunwise direction, and some parties were known to make three clockwise passes around the yard for added blessings and protection. Fishermen were also known to follow this practice, leaving the harbor and directing their boats clockwise whenever possible.

HOW TO USE IT

With any action you're thinking of beginning, it's always best if you start out in a clockwise direction. This can encompass anything from the course you take when you set places for dinner and the route you choose to pass papers around a conference table to the path you follow when massaging your sweetheart's back. Preparing food (mixing ingredients or stirring a sauce) should always be done in a clockwise manner. If you're having bad luck at the card table, getting up and circling your chair like a planet around the sun is a known way of reversing your luck. And turning around in place three times clockwise is an effective antidote to almost anything unlucky.

COAL

WHY IT IS LUCKY

Although when thinking about lucky objects one doesn't automatically think, *Ah, yes! Of course! Coal!* it is, nevertheless, a tried-and-true good-luck charm. Beginning in the nineteenth century, burglars were known to carry around a lump when embarking on a new project, to keep them safe from detection.* Soldiers were known to carry coal with them into battle, and sailors, on sea voyages. While in the United States children are warned that if they misbehave they will receive nothing but coal for Christmas, in the United Kingdom coal is an essential part of the "First Footing" ritual. The belief is that the first person to step foot in a house on New Year's Day should come bearing a lucky gift of coal, which is then burned in the fire while the recipient makes a wish. It will bring the house dweller luck throughout the year.

HOW TO USE IT

Grab a lump and put it in your pocket. Finding a piece of coal on the ground is considered lucky, although it is recommended that you either spit on the coal before pocketing it or toss it over your left shoulder and leave it behind; the luck will follow you either way.

....

Of course, the reliability of such a charm is questionable, as most reports of this custom came from burglars who had been arrested.

COINS

WHY THEY ARE LUCKY

Lucky traditions related to coins reach back to times when people believed mercurial gods oversaw their lives and paying tribute to these deities by tossing coins away was habitual. Gods of the sea, who were believed to control many aspects of ancient life, were apparently just as happy for people to fling coins into a fountain as into the sea itself, and the practice of throwing coins into wells to keep them from running dry became common as far back as ancient Greece.

HOW TO USE THEM

Always carry a penny in your pocket for good luck. See if you can't find one with your birth year for an extra oomph. If you find a penny (especially if it is heads side up), pick it up; it means more are to follow. Some say that finding a penny after a rainstorm is particularly lucky, as it likely fell from heaven. Pennies stored in a jar in the kitchen will attract good luck. Toss a coin (or, better yet, three) into a well or fountain for general luck. Turning a coin over in your pocket at the sight of the new moon will guarantee your financial success all month long. A coin with a hole in it (associated with the shells and pebbles worn as necklaces by sea gods) or one that is bent will bring good luck.

CRICKET

WHY IT IS LUCKY

It is almost universally agreed that crickets are harbingers of good fortune, chiefly regarding financial concerns. Throughout time, they could be found chirping inside homes, often near the warmest spot in the house, the hearth. As a result, they have come to be seen as the embodiment of cheerfulness and a contented household. In China, small cages were built to house crickets so they could be kept inside to assure continued luck and even transported so that luck would go wherever they did. It is also believed by some that crickets can predict the weather (by chirping louder at the approach of rain), foretell death (by hopping away), and warn of the approach of a stranger (by ceasing to make noise). Charms in the form of crickets can be found in many ancient cultures around the world and are said to be highly effective in warding off the evil eye.

HOW TO USE IT

No action is required here; just don't kill it, which is sure to bring bad luck, in the form of anything from comrade crickets tracking you down and eating your socks to certain death.

CROOKEDNESS

WHY IT IS LUCKY

For many, crooked things carry a negative connotation and evoke mental images of corrupt politicians and businessmen on the take. But in the world of luck, when something is crooked, it is filled with lucky potential. A crooked horseshoe nail and a crooked pin are both lucky to find; crooked sticks were once thought to be excellent kitchen aids (one kept by the side of the hearth was thought to prevent the cook from ruining the meal); and farmers were known to plow in crooked patterns to keep evil spirits on their toes. Damaged coins (called "crooked," "bent," or "bowed") have been considered lucky since the sixteenth century; what kind of coin they are doesn't seem to matter. They can be held onto as personal luck charms, left as offerings for saints, or tossed away when making a wish. A crooked coin is sure to bring luck to the person who carries it in his pocket, heal the person who stashes it under her pillow, and should never be parted with if bad luck is to be kept at bay.

HOW TO USE IT

If you spot something crooked, go ahead and pick it up. Some sources say if you're going to keep it, the object is best stowed in your left pocket. If you have a highly pressing wish to make, throw that bent coin into a fountain and wish away.

DARUMA

WHY IT IS LUCKY

Armless, legless, and eyeless, on paper the Daruma doll doesn't sound that appealing, and yet he is a popular mascot of good luck. Named after the founder of Zen Buddhism, the Bodhidharma, the Daruma is ubiquitous in Japan and, more recently, has become popular in the United States. Hollow and made out of papier-mâché or ceramic, and with a round shape and low center of gravity, the Daruma is like a Weeble—it wobbles but it doesn't fall down—and, as a result, is a symbol of steadfastness and persistence in the face of adversity. The unpainted eyes are a blank slate on which the owner can paint his wishes. The first eye is filled in upon purchase, with a specific goal or wish in mind; the second eye is filled in only upon its achievement.

HOW TO USE IT

If you're finding you have a difficult task at hand or are embarking on a new venture, go out and get a Daruma. Although they come in many sizes, there's no evidence that a bigger one will bring better results, so buy whatever size fits the size of your desire (or apartment). A Daruma purchased for yourself or a friend on January 1 is the perfect representation of a New Year's resolution. When the goal is achieved, the second eye can be painted, and the Daruma can be displayed proudly as a sign of accomplishment.

DRESSING FOR LUCK

WHY IT IS LUCKY

Many believe that wearing a certain shirt can positively affect the outcome of a sporting event or that a particular item of clothing will bring luck on important occasions. And this is nothing new; lucky beliefs have been attached to clothing since we traded in our fig leaves. It has long been considered good luck to put on any item of clothing inside out (or front to back). A new item of clothing should always be recognized and made lucky by putting a penny in the pocket or sewing a coin into a seam (a process called "handseling"). It is considered good luck to wear new clothes (or at least one new item of clothing) for New Year's, Christmas, and particularly Easter—it encourages the luck gods to provide you with more new clothing.

HOW TO USE IT

Always begin dressing by putting your right arm into a shirt or your right leg into a pair of pants. Avoid doing up your buttons incorrectly. If you do, remove the item of clothing entirely and start over. If you find you've put something on inside out, leave it that way and wear it all day; it will bring you luck. To reverse bad luck, turn your hat front to back or your underwear inside out. If you attribute your luck to a certain item of clothing, keep wearing it and don't wash it until the luck runs out.

ELEPHANT

WHY IT IS LUCKY

Even though your chances of encountering an elephant are slim, crossing paths with one is thought to be very lucky. Considered among the wisest creatures in the animal kingdom, they are known for their prodigious memory as well as their phenomenal strength, and the belief in their lucky powers stems from the admiration these beasts have inspired for centuries and all over the globe. They are especially prized in Hindu culture, where Ganesha, the beloved god of wisdom and good luck, appears in the form of an elephant-headed being and is known for his capacity to bestow favors, chiefly in the areas of business and financial enterprise.

HOW TO USE IT

Wearing a charm in the form of an elephant will transfer to the wearer the animal's characteristics, including wisdom and the ability to move obstacles out of the way (metaphorically speaking, that is). Some believe that wearing a bracelet or ring made out of the hair from an elephant's tail will bring good luck. A statue of an elephant may be placed outside the entrance of a home (facing the doorway) to protect it from anyone or anything with evil intentions, and to bring good fortune. Although there are different schools of thought on the matter, it appears that the ornamental animal's tusks may be up or down; when up the luck is caught and held, when down the luck is allowed to flow freely.

FINGER CROSSING

WHY IT IS LUCKY

The common explanation for the power and prevalence of this gesture is said to be related to the early Christians. Not allowed to worship Christ in public, his followers showed secret solidarity by crossing their fingers. Some have dismissed this notion on the grounds that the shape created by crossed fingers bears no relationship to an actual cross and that the late appearance of the gesture (the earliest references aren't found until the late nineteenth century) suggests this explanation has been applied only in retrospect. Perhaps a more satisfying theory offers the belief that a wish or a lie can be held captive at the point where the two fingers meet. The wish is held until it comes true, the lie trapped and therefore able to escape detection.

HOW TO USE IT

We all probably know too well that fingers should be crossed when telling a lie to mitigate bad behavior. However, you can also cross your fingers (the index and middle ones) when making a wish or to ward off bad luck in a plethora of situations (when walking under a ladder, passing by a cemetery, or otherwise tempting fate). If you have a friend with you, you can redouble your wishing efforts as they did in bygone days by forming a cross with your index finger and the index finger of another. One of you makes a wish, while the other wishes you well.

FOUR-LEAF CLOVER

WHY IT IS LUCKY

Other than their scarcity, there doesn't seem to be any tangible reason why four-leaf clovers are lucky, although it appears that even the Druids were down on their hands and knees looking for them. They believed that these tiny plants were effective protectors against malevolent beings and would render these beings visible, enabling the Druids to see through their trickery. Even though Eve, who ostensibly brought one out of the Garden of Eden with her, had a bit of a bumpy ride, four-leaf clovers developed an association with love and marriage, and, once found, were known to summon a marriage prospect within the day. More generally, each leaf is imbued with a distinct significance: the first brings "fame," the second "wealth," the third a "faithful lover," and the last "glorious health."

HOW TO USE IT

Although it is possible to buy mass-produced four-leaf clovers almost anywhere, the most potent ones will be found the old-fashioned way. If you happen to spot one, keep it for yourself to bring prosperity, or give it away to a friend or lover as a token of devotion and a harbinger of fortune. Place it inside your shoe and the next person you meet (given your gender preference) will be your future mate.

THE GOLDEN POO

WHY IT IS LUCKY

In 1999, the president of a Japanese company that manufactures gift items had the brilliant idea to create a golden luck charm in the shape of a perfect little poo. Measuring just under a half an inch tall, these charms became fashionable with schoolgirls and then hit the proverbial fan to become sought after by everyone from businessmen to grandmothers. Since their first release, more than 2 million little golden turds have been sold. Why poo, of all things, you ask? Well, the charm is called *Kin no Unko* (the Golden Poo) in Japanese, and the word *unko* (poo) is a homonym for the word that means "luck."* In the United Kingdom, poo has a longer history of lucky associations. Dating back to the seventeenth century, stepping in livestock poo (aka manure) was considered lucky, as was having a bird poo on you. And in France, it is considered good luck to step in dog poo with your left foot. Really, it's only fair that there be some upside.

HOW TO USE IT

These charms can be worn on bracelets, necklaces, or dangled from a cell phone. It might not be your thing, but given that it seems to work for 2 million others, it's nothing to pooh-pooh.

....

Apparently in Japan poo is only lucky when it's golden. A book released there called Cleaning the Toilet to Attract Luck *explains why a good scrub brush and some Clorox will help bring luck into your life.*

HANDS

WHY THEY ARE LUCKY

The hand plays a significant role in our lives as the symbol of a promise or intention. We seal a deal with a handshake, give our hand in marriage, and pledge allegiance with our hand over our heart. Charms in the shape of hands have been worn for luck and protection since ancient times, including the Arabic *Hamsa* or Hebrew *Hamesh* hand. Burglars have availed themselves of the lucky power of hands by creating their own charm—the Hand of Glory. Starting in the Middle Ages, the hand of a hanged criminal would be severed from the body, pickled, and dried, and then a candle (made from wax, the fat of, apparently, any hanged man, and sesame) was stuck in it, and the whole inglorious mess was brought on thieving expeditions.

HOW TO USE THEM

Stick with an attractive charm and a line of work that doesn't include the fear of arrest. Rubbing the hands of someone who has recently had a run of good luck is thought to transfer luck. The right hand is always preferred for any activity (sorry, lefties!), and if you accidentally shake hands with the same person twice, do it a third time to ward off bad luck. You can also use your right hand to make the sign of the horn (stick out your little finger and index finger while folding the thumb and other fingers onto your palm) or the fig (curl your fingers down while sticking your thumb out between the middle and index fingers) to ward off the evil eye.

HORN

WHY IT IS LUCKY

The horns from animals such as oxen, rams, bulls, antelopes, and stags are known in many different countries as symbols of fertility and plenty. In Italy, where they are called *cornos* and are hugely popular, horns are thought to bring prosperity and to protect against the evil eye.

HOW TO USE IT

Mounted on a wall, horns will bring luck to a home or the owner of a business. A horn charm worn around a man's neck or carried in his pocket is said to increase sex appeal and virility and provide protection against curses that might be directed at his "manliness." A variety of horn charms exist, including a version that looks like an antelope horn, as well as a red plastic version that looks like a pepper and is called a *chili corno*. Male or female, if you need protection from the evil eye and you don't happen to be wearing a horn charm, you can always make the sign of the horn (*mano cornuto*) with your right hand by sticking out your little finger and your index finger while folding your thumb and your other fingers onto your palm. It's the gestural equivalent of the school yard saying, "I'm rubber, you're glue. Whatever you say bounces off me and sticks to you," and shoots the bad luck right back at the sender.

HORSE CHESTNUTS

WHY THEY ARE LUCKY

It is generally assumed that the name *horse chestnut* comes from the fact that these nuts were, a long, long time ago, given as food and medicine to horses. In the United States they are commonly called buckeyes, as the partly opened side is said to resemble the eye of a male deer. It's difficult to say how exactly the horse chestnut became associated with luck. Most explanations suggest it is related to the reputation the trees have of being extremely long-lived. The nuts were fed to domesticated animals in the belief that "like brings like"; feed an animal something with a long life, the animal in turn will have a long life. Eventually the nuts were believed to pass along the characteristics of health, longevity, and therefore luck to the folks who turned their blossoms into tea or simply carried them around on their person.

HOW TO USE THEM

Be warned: horse chestnuts are poisonous when raw and should only be ingested (by you or your horse) when prepared under the supervision of someone who actually knows what they are doing. That's not us. Less risky: simply place one in your pocket and carry it around with you to bring good luck.

HORSESHOE

WHY IT IS LUCKY

The horseshoe is the trifecta of lucky charms, and here's why: It is associated with horses, long thought to be magical animals and linked to good fortune in almost every country around the world. Horseshoes were originally made from iron, an ancient metal believed to carry protective powers because of its ability to withstand fire. In some countries, even blacksmiths were thought to possess mystical abilities, since they wielded control over this seemingly supernatural element. Finally, the U or crescent shape has long been seen as a capable protector against evil and is manifest in sacred structures around the world, including the arches that fill churches, temples, and mosques, and in the arrangement of stones at Stonehenge.

HOW TO USE IT

A horseshoe is considered to be most lucky when it is found by accident, open hoof space toward you, with the holes from seven nails. It's a bonus if any nails remain in place. Hang the horseshoe over a doorway of your home, inside or outside. It can be hung with the prongs either up or down, since there is no consensus as to which way attracts good fortune better. If you hang the horseshoe with the prongs up, it acts as a storage container to collect all the good luck floating around (the more widely accepted practice). If you hang it prongs down, the good luck will flow out and surround the home.

HUNCHBACK

WHY IT IS LUCKY

Although today it seems terribly impolite to speak of, historically hunchback sightings were considered to be lucky, particularly if the viewer was actually able to reach out and rub the hunchback's hump. It was long believed that a person with a deformity had the ability to scare evil spirits away or disable them in peals of laughter. Kings and pharaohs were known to retain personal hunchbacks to keep evil at bay and ensure good luck. Since that wasn't practical for the average Joe, touching became the next best thing. Given the prevalence of the belief, some with the deformity were able to capitalize on this practice and earn a bit of income by charging interested parties. It is said that in Paris players in the stock market were especially susceptible to this belief, and some even say that the word *hunch* comes from the association between good fortune and the hunchback. Italians today are known for their belief in the power of the hunchback and fashion charms called *gobbos*—after Lancelot Gobbo in Shakespeare's *Merchant of Venice*—that resemble exaggerated hunchbacks in miniature.

HOW TO USE IT

Trying to touch a stranger is never recommended. If you feel this lucky practice is for you (and who are we to judge?), go out and buy a charm; they are widely available.

JATUKHAM RAMATHEP

WHY IT IS LUCKY

Sometimes, like in the case of a tabloid celebrity, the frenzy around something seems disproportionate to the inherent qualities of the thing itself. This seems to be the case with the craze surrounding the Jatukham Ramathep charm in Thailand, which has reached such a peak that dozens were injured and a woman trampled to death at a temple while trying to get their hands on the lucky amulets. Originally created in 1987 by a shrine in conjunction with a policeman who claimed to have access to divine powers, the amulet shows the figure of Jatukham Ramathep seated with his right knee raised. Although no one can really explain why the figure is lucky, many believe he is the conflation of two historical Thai princes. The original charms were modestly sized (less than two inches in diameter) and cost about thirty-nine baht (one dollar and twenty-five cents). Today there are more than four hundred different versions, with starting prices of around three hundred baht (ten dollars) and some versions priced at a million baht (thirty thousand dollars). A Thai economic research center has estimated that the yearly revenue of the charms, which includes a cottage industry of related books and merchandise, could reach the equivalent of half the amount of Thailand's biggest export—rice.

HOW TO USE IT

Well, buy one if you like, but avoid the crush and order it online.

KNOCKING ON WOOD

WHY IT IS LUCKY

This tradition dates back to pagan times, when people believed that gods dwelled in trees. Touching wood (if you're British) or knocking on wood was a way of acknowledging and securing favor with the gods. People have also long believed that if you draw attention to your good fortune ("I looked so hot in those jeans last night"), you will make evil spirits envious and they will take it away ("I gained ten pounds and can't even fit into my jeans"); "He who talks too much of happiness summons grief" goes the old proverb. There are two theories as to why knocking on wood helps: One explanation suggests that knocking on wood frightens the bad spirits away or prevents them from hearing of your good fortune. The other proposes that it acknowledges and calls to the good spirits, who will use their power to ensure you retain your good luck.

HOW TO USE IT

Knocking on wood is largely used as a preventative measure and should always be done after talking about good things that you expect will come your way. You only have to do it once, but some people knock three times just to be safe. Superstitions aside, it's probably less annoying to your friends if you knock on wood after bragging; a little humility is always appreciated.

KNOT

WHY IT IS LUCKY

Although some interactions with knots are riddled with frustration, they have historically been thought of as sources of good luck, protection, and divination, and ancient beliefs suggest wishes can be captured and retained by them. They have been tied into clothing by gamblers and sailors to bring good fortune, woven with ribbons into girls' hair or horses' manes for protection (the evil spirits get trapped in the spot where the knot is tied), and worked into wedding bouquets to capture and hold happiness.

HOW TO USE IT

In life's passages (births and deaths) it's important that nothing be knotted (bedclothes, shoelaces, etc.) to obstruct a smooth transition. Although not for the clumsy, a groom can prevent unwanted complications on his wedding night by walking down the aisle with one shoelace untied. If you haven't yet found Mr. Right, travel to a different country and tie nine knots in your stockings or socks while reciting:

*"This knot I knit, / This knot I tie, / To see my love as he goes by, /
In his apparel and array, / As he walks in every day,"*

then stick them under your pillow. You'll see your future lover soon thereafter. To test a relationship, tie some grass in a knot and think of the person you love. If the grass stays tied, the relationship will last. If not, grab your passport, some socks, and head for the border.

LADY LUCK

WHY SHE IS LUCKY

There are lots of old ladies hanging around Las Vegas these days, but the one everyone wants to run into is Lady Luck. More than two thousand years old, Fortuna (for the ancient Romans) was the original lucky lady, and she personified chance and fortune. Although she wasn't lucky enough to be granted her own feast day, she did have her own cult, along with a number of temples that became destination oracles for emperors in search of answers. Priestesses there gave seekers responses to questions as the result of die tosses or lot drawings. Representations of her on coins and carvings are plentiful and varied. She is often pictured with a cornucopia, symbolizing the possibility of plenty, and sometimes with a rudder or with a wheel, where the touch of her hand steers man's fate. And she's often shown blindfolded or standing on or juggling a ball to show the fickle nature and unpredictability of her beneficence.

HOW TO USE HER

Like any lady, treat her with respect. Don't assume she'll always be there when you need her, be grateful when she makes an appearance, and always remember to give her credit when credit is due. And don't forget the Latin proverb, which is about as old as she is: *Fortis fortuna adiuvat.* "Fortune favors the bold."

MANEKI NEKO

WHY IT IS LUCKY

Before Hello Kitty there was the Maneki Neko (Beckoning Cat), a Japanese sculpture commonly placed in businesses or homes to attract good luck. The cats are usually shown with one raised paw, which causes some confusion in the United States. Although Americans beckon with the backs of their hands facing outward, the Japanese beckon with their palms facing outward, which explains why many people in the West mistakenly think the cat is waving, not beckoning. Regardless, left paw up attracts customers, right paw up attracts money, and most of the cats are wearing a collar with a bell while grasping a gold coin or fish with their lowered paw. Although rarely mentioned by name, the earliest Maneki Neko–like statues can be dated to the Edo period in the seventeenth century.

HOW TO USE IT

Decide what kind of luck you want to draw, and then take your pick of the litter. Traditional versions include calico (red, brown, and black), the rarest cat in real life and the most popular style; black, which is said to ward off evil and is thought to be highly useful for women with unwanted admirers; and white, which symbolizes purity. In addition there are modern variations of gold (for money) and pink (for love).

MASCOT

WHY IT IS LUCKY

A mascot can be pretty much anything—an animal, object, person, or design—which is then taken to be the embodiment of the luck of a team, business, political entity, or any group. The word *mascot* comes from the French Provençal *masco*, which means "sorceress"; through its own magic, the mascot is believed to keep witches and any other evil spirits at bay. The role of the mascot reaches as far back as the ancient Egyptians, who had their snakes; Zeus, who had his eagle; and the Chinese, who had their dragons. As repositories of luck, they are rallying points for any kind of team and, it is said, only fail to do their job if the recipient is unworthy. Sorry, Cubs fans, you have no one to blame but yourselves.

HOW TO USE IT

Choose wisely, because once you've committed to a mascot, it's best to stick with it. If you choose a particular thing to be your mascot (say, that one-eyed bunny stuffed animal you've had since childhood), guard it carefully; the loss of a mascot can be detrimental to the luck of those who value it. If you're feeling doubly in need of luck, you can stroke your mascot or even kiss it, although, depending on what it is, you might first want to make sure no one else is around.

MOJO

WHY IT IS LUCKY

Although Austin Powers has many of us convinced that a man's mojo exists just below his belt buckle, mojo is more accurately described as a red flannel bag filled with bones, roots, or symbolic objects that can aid in casting a spell and protect or bring the wearer luck. A mojo bag (also known as a mojo hand) is one of the fundamental good-luck charms of Hoodoo and Conjure traditions, which are a mixture of African, European, and Native American religious, magical, and folklore practices, melded together in slave communities in the American South. Locating, obtaining, and keeping mojo was a preoccupation of lovers and gamblers, and references to mojo pop up frequently in blues songs, such as Blind Lemon Jefferson's "Low Down Mojo Blues" and Preston Foster's "I Got My Mojo Working." Today, the term *mojo* is used more loosely to describe that ineffable thing that gives a person sexual charisma.

HOW TO USE IT

Mojo bags can be created for any occasion and any need. You can customize one to bring yourself luck in love, gambling, business, lawsuits, and just about anything else under the sun. Once you've created your mojo, be sure it is not visible; it can be pinned inside of your clothing or secreted in an appropriate spot where it will be best suited to work its magic.

MONEY

WHY IT IS LUCKY

The relationship between money and luck is best understood through the concept of "handsel," which has at its root the belief that what begins well will continue well. Or, more specifically, what starts lucky will remain lucky. As a result, the first use of something is considered notably auspicious and must be honored. Inaugurating the beginning of something with money, whether it is an item of clothing, a life, or a trip, is "handseling" it, ensuring its luck from the start. Related is the idea of "luck money," which reaches back to nineteenth-century financial transactions when the *seller* gave money to the *buyer* after the purchase price had been paid "for luck." The idea was to bolster the transaction as lucky, secure the luck of both participants in the deal, and ensure that the whole thing wouldn't go south.

HOW TO USE IT

If you give someone a new purse or wallet, always tuck some money into it (even something as small as a penny); it means the recipient will never be without. Give someone a coin to wear in a new item of clothing (or put one in your own) and the garment will always bring luck when worn. Toss a penny overboard at the beginning of a sea voyage to ensure a safe passage. And brides, put a penny in your shoe on your wedding day. Grooms, if you actually give her the penny, it will guarantee the marriage will be highly successful.

OMAMORI

WHY THEY ARE LUCKY

The dawn of the New Year is an important occasion and the perfect time to think concertedly about the future. The New Year in Japan brings the beginning of Oshogatsu, a period of three days that is arguably the most significant moment in the New Year's cycle and a critical time to get your lucky ducks in a row. During this time the Japanese flock to temples and shrines, where they purchase lucky charms called *omamori* to pray for an auspicious year. *Omamori* are small objects contained within often elaborately decorated paper or fabric packets that bear inscriptions to protect their owners from bad luck. There are many different types of *omamori* that can be purchased, each addressing a different lucky desire, such as success in money matters, love, or exams.

HOW TO USE THEM

Although they're most popular at New Year's, you don't have to wait to purchase *omamori*; they can be bought and used during any time of need (and many shrines deliver). As times have changed, so have *omamori*, and now charms can be purchased to ward off everything from car accidents to major technological woes. Although *omamori* can be left at a shrine as an offering, they can also be kept and worn on a key ring, dangled from a cell phone, or hung from the collar of a pet.

PALAD KHIK

WHY IT IS LUCKY

Sometimes translated as "honorable surrogate penis," the *palad khik* is a Thai charm worn by men around their waist that, similarly to the Italian *corno*, is believed to bring luck in love and protection against evil spirits, primarily those whose influence is directed south of the Mason-Dixon Line. The charm is said to have its origins in the Sanskrit *linga*, which, when translated literally means "sign" or "mark," but is used to describe symbols of male and female sex organs, often associated with the Hindu god Shiva. Many variations of the *palad khik* are available and include versions with penises ridden by crouching animals, women, or the twelve signs of the zodiac. And these charms aren't the only places penises pop up around Thailand. The Lingam (or Tuptim) Shrine in Bangkok is an apparent hotbed of phalluses, and bar owners are said to tap a *palad khik* on the tables of their female dancers to insure a financially successful evening.

HOW TO USE IT

Put a little swash below your buckle and buy a *palad khik*. Multiple *palad khik* can be worn at the same time to bring good luck in different areas of your life, including love, gambling, and financial matters, and although not regularly worn by women, they are thought to be effective charms against purse snatchers.

PIG

WHY IT IS LUCKY

The pig is a long-standing symbol of good fortune, which may have at its root the simple explanation that, in agrarian societies, owning a pig was often crucial to a family's economic well-being. Once considered an Irish family's most valuable asset, "the gentleman who pays the rent" has been made into charms that are still popular in Ireland, although some believe a small portion of the charm must be broken off to ensure good luck. For Germans, pigs and luck are inextricably linked; to say you've experienced good luck in German you say *Schwein gehabt* (You had a pig). For the Chinese, the pig is a symbol of honesty and diligence, and a pig statue in the home is thought to bring happiness, prosperity, and good luck.

HOW TO USE IT

Buy a piggy bank to store your money in—it will not only safeguard what money you have but will also attract more. Every human resources person should know that a statue of a golden pig placed on the CEO's desk ensures a dedicated workforce. Many believe it's good luck to greet the New Year with a pig, so if you're not up to actually roasting one, you can buy little marzipan pigs, often accompanied by marzipan mushrooms, as is the German custom, and serve them to your guests.

PIN

WHY IT IS LUCKY

It would seem that practically everyone has heard the rhyme "See a pin and pick it up, all the day you'll have good luck," or some variation, since there are many. Although the rhyme doesn't appear until the mid-nineteenth century, as early as the seventeenth century people were being exhorted not to pass pins by. Pins have historically been associated with witchcraft (think voodoo dolls) and, as potentially blood-drawing objects, were seen as dangerous. Although these associations may have guided the list of prohibitions regarding them, the pressure to pick up pins is likely related to the old saying "He that will not stoop for a pin will never be worth a pound," a simple reflection of societal values placed on economy and thrift.

HOW TO USE IT

The point is (sorry, bad pun), if you see one, pick it up. It appears it's best if the pin is head side facing you. Don't ever lend or give a pin to a friend; it will injure the relationship. If someone does make the mistake of giving you a pin, do not say thank you, and give a coin in exchange as an antidote. Pins can be thrown into wells to bring good luck, particularly if you're looking for a mate. And a pin taken from a bride's dress can bring about a wedding for the pin pincher.

RABBIT'S FOOT

WHY IT IS LUCKY

First we have to clear up one thing. There are rabbits and there are hares, and they are not the same animal, although the lore around the rabbit's foot has conflated the two. Born with their eyes open, hares have long been believed to have exceedingly effective protective powers (for example, second sight), although their feet are nothing to write home about. Rabbits, born hairless and blind, have themselves been historically admired for their procreative powers. If you were a farmer who needed to populate your house with able bodies to help in the fields, wouldn't you envy them? Also impressive were their overactive hindquarters. It did not escape notice that their back feet touched the ground before their front feet while running (a highly unusual but very effective method) and that these furry thumpers, not the front ones, were also the primary instruments for burrowing holes. As a result, it was the hind feet that were ascribed with lucky powers.

HOW TO USE IT

If you plan to carry one of these furry feet around with you, it's most efficacious if it is the left hind paw (although we have no idea how you'll know). Some lore suggests that, further to this, the paw must be from an animal that has been killed during a full moon by a cross-eyed person. Front foot or back, straight-eyed or crossed, it should always be carried in your left-hand pocket.

"RABBITS, RABBITS, RABBITS"

WHY IT IS LUCKY

Hares and rabbits have long been associated with luck, and many people believe that to say "rabbits, rabbits, rabbits" on the first morning of every month is to bring four weeks of good fortune and, more immediately, a gift. Variations exist, with some believing the saying should go "white rabbits, white rabbits, white rabbits" and others "hares, hares, hares."

HOW TO USE IT

Choose whichever version of the saying feels most natural (we know, none feel *natural*), and say it first thing in the morning, on the first day of the month, before any other words have been said. If you're not prone to dizziness, some believe it is even more beneficial if you spin around three times in place while saying it. Make sure you don't get confused and say "black rabbit, black rabbit, black rabbit" by mistake, as bad luck will follow.

RED THREAD

WHY IT IS LUCKY

Sometimes things are considered lucky simply because they are believed to prevent bad things from happening. Such is at least partially the case with red thread, which has, for many years, been known to provide protection against evil spirits. The color red, associated with strength, passion, and vitality, is believed to be a valuable protector against witchcraft and more generic evildoers, and thread is a practical vehicle for attaching this lucky color to things in need of fortification. Similarly, the Chinese believe that tying certain objects with red thread will animate them with chi, life's lucky energy, and the ancient practice of feng shui relies heavily on an accurate object–red thread–corner-of-the-room-placement combination to get the chi flowing.

HOW TO USE IT

Children are thought to benefit from wearing a red ribbon or thread, as are farm animals, especially cattle. To bring luck to a child, tie red ribbons to his crib or stroller or weave them into her hair. If you want to protect an animal, tie a red thread around its horn or its tail. Red thread can also be worn while gambling or be tied into the interior of a new car.

SEVEN

WHY IT IS LUCKY

Although odd numbers are generally believed to be luckier than even ones, the number seven stands out as having particularly lucky properties, which it brings to anything it is associated with. Since at least as far back as ancient Babylon, seven has had special significance. Ancient Greeks considered it to be a "perfect" number; the Japanese have seven lucky gods; and it is a critical number throughout the Bible and in Jewish mysticism. There are seven graces, seven heavens, seven seas, seven ages of man, and the list goes on. Dating back to the thirteenth century, a seventh son was believed to have the gift of special sight and healing powers. And, in the game of craps, seven is the luckiest roll you can have.*

HOW TO USE IT

Try applying it to any part of your life—from the number of things you purchase, to the date you plan for an event, to the number you pick for your jersey on a sports team—and it's sure to bring good luck.

At least as your first roll, but not if you've already rolled a nine, for example, which then becomes your point, in which case you have to roll another nine before you roll a seven or else it's a seven out and you lose. So, actually, it's not always good. Got it?

SHOES

WHY THEY ARE LUCKY

There are a number of superstitions regarding shoes, but perhaps the most prevalent is, oddly enough, the belief that throwing an old shoe after someone will bring them good luck, especially when they're embarking on a journey or at the end of a wedding ceremony. Although there is no consensus as to how the tradition began or why it was believed effective, old shoes were invested with symbolic import (particularly regarding financial transactions) by everyone from the ancient Assyrians to the Anglo-Saxons. Some suggest the throwing of the shoe at a wedding is a symbol of the transfer of ownership and power ("You're taking my daughter, here, have my shoe, too"), although there is little evidence to support this hypothesis. More credible is the suggestion that shoes were just generally believed lucky and that weddings seemed an appropriate time to take advantage of that.

HOW TO USE THEM

Please note, that's throwing a shoe *after* someone, not *at* someone. And this also does not mean that pairs of shoes should be tossed like rice as the bride and groom leave the wedding ceremony. Safer is to tie the shoe to the back of the departing couple's car, another long-standing tradition. More generally, it is unlucky to give shoes as a gift for Christmas, to burn them, or to place them atop a table.

SPIDER

WHY IT IS LUCKY

Although when arachnophobes think *spider* they also think *get the can of Raid!*, spiders have long been considered lucky, and the sighting of one in your home or on your person, auspicious. Very small spiders, called "money spiders" or "money spinners," were thought to bring wealth to whomever they landed on, especially if they were seen dropping from the ceiling (and the effect was magnified if the spider was red). A spider found on clothing was a sign that the person would soon receive a new outfit. Although some explain that the relationship between spiders and luck reaches back to the heroic roles spiders played in a variety of legends dating to early Christianity, others believe the multitalented and resourceful creature is, legends aside, simply a worthy conduit of luck. And besides, who really needs Raid when you have a spider? They can kill plenty of other insects and are a lot luckier.

HOW TO USE IT

Although many believe it's enough to spot the spider, others believe the spider should be put in your pocket, tossed over your left shoulder, or eaten (gross). The problem these rituals present is that it's very unlucky to kill a spider. "If you want to live and thrive, let the spider go alive" goes the old proverb, and good luck will only be bestowed on those who live and let live. So it's probably best to just leave it alone.

SPITTING

WHY IT IS LUCKY

Although most of us have been taught that it is impolite, spitting has long been associated with good luck, protection, and the way to emphasize an oath or promise. Some lore suggests that the spit represents a small piece of the soul, which is well spent currying the favor of the gods. The ancient Greeks were known to spit on their hands for good luck in gambling. Fishermen spit into their nets before lowering them into the water. Boxers often spit on their fists or gloves before a fight. And although there are practical reasons for spitting on one's hands before gripping a tool, there are thought to be ancillary benefits as well.

HOW TO USE IT

There's virtually nothing that can't be improved upon with a little spit. You can spit on: money you receive, just "for luck"; dice, to help roll the right number; your hand (before shaking someone else's), to cement a deal; an exam paper or lottery ticket. Spitting is also a great antidote to evil spirits or actions. Avail yourself of your salivary glands after walking under a ladder, to ward off the evil eye, or if a black cat crosses your path. Although it may require more coordination and shouldn't be done into the wind, spitting over your shoulder is another way to reverse bad fortune.

TATTOO

WHY IT IS LUCKY

The 1991 discovery of a tattooed iceman on the Italian-Austrian border suggests that human beings have been marking their skin for at least 5,200 years. Ancient peoples as diverse as the Egyptians, Greeks and Romans, Native Americans, and Polynesians all practiced forms of body adornment, with techniques, designs, colors, and placement varying widely. The motives that drove the practice then appear to be as diverse as they are today, with rationales ranging from pure decoration to social identification to drawing in luck. Sailors and coal miners, employed in especially dangerous professions, have been historical believers that tattoos would help bring them good fortune, and often bore images of anchors or lanterns. Today's tattooed, many occupying jobs that are only dangerously boring, sport images of everything from traditional good-luck charms such as horseshoes and four-leaf clovers to more idiosyncratic or personalized lucky choices. And some choose to fly in the face of fate by wearing images of a black cat or the number thirteen.

HOW TO USE IT

Get inked! Just bear in mind that no tattoo that gets infected, no matter what it's of, is lucky, so get a recommendation and choose a reputable artist who works in a safe, clean studio. Be sure to pick a subject that is, and will remain, significant for you, since tattoos are, after all, a lifelong commitment.

TIKI

WHY IT IS LUCKY

Remember that episode of the *Brady Bunch* when they go to Hawaii because Mike has a job there and one of the construction workers finds a tiki idol and, ignoring the warnings of a wise old man, tosses the tiki onto the grass where Bobby picks it up and puts it on a string to wear as a good-luck charm around his neck and then he is almost crushed by a hideous wall-hanging in their hotel room and then Alice wears the tiki during a hula lesson and hurts her back and then Bobby gives it to Greg for luck while he's surfing and Greg wipes out on a creampuff roller and practically drowns and then Peter takes it and is almost attacked by a hairy spider and then they decide to return the tiki to the ancient burial ground and an archaeologist played by Vincent Price traps them in a cave because he thinks they're trying to steal all of his treasures? Well, that's all that most of us know about tikis. But according to Polynesian mythology, Tiki was the first man, and tikis, more properly called *hei-tiki* (*hei* signifying neck ornament), were carvings created and worn by the Maori. Traditionally made out of a hard green stone, they were squat figures with oversized heads usually cocked to one side. Although the original Maori intention of the *hei-tiki* is not known, today they are worn for luck and protection.

HOW TO USE IT

Get one, wear it, and grab a wave. Just make sure you don't pick it up from a construction site.

TOPPING-OUT

WHY IT IS LUCKY

Topping-out begins when the final and highest element (usually a beam) of a newly constructed building is ready to be put into place. After it has been welded and secured, a small pine tree is affixed to it, symbolizing a job completed in safety and promising good luck for future inhabitants. The earliest references to topping-out date back to around AD 700 in Scandinavia, where, as the legend goes, structures were built and then topped with grain for the Norse god Odin's horse. Odin was so pleased with the care given to his trusty steed that he rewarded the builders and all future dwellers with good fortune. The tradition spread with the Norse around Europe and was modified according to the vegetation readily available to the builders. Not unrelated were ancient ceremonies that developed around the laying of the cornerstone of a building, often accompanied by a human sacrifice. Today, trees are often replaced with flags, and both the topping-out and cornerstone rituals have become ribbon-cutting ceremonies and other sources of more modern fanfare.

HOW TO USE IT

Topping-out is appropriate for any new structure being built, including a home or doghouse, so if you've reached the end of a new construction project, don't forget to secure good luck by affixing a little greenery to the top. No human sacrifice required.

UNDERWEAR

WHY IT IS LUCKY

It's not just in the modern age that men are preoccupied with what's going on under women's dresses. Since the mid-nineteenth century, an undergarment put on inside out was generally thought to be lucky, although not doing the catches, laces, or hooks up properly was a sure sign the day would be a bad one. The sight of a woman's petticoat peeping out from under her clothing was believed to be an indication that her father loved her more than her mother did. And an untied garter (or any other item of clothing that might slip down) was a sign that a lover was thinking of her.

HOW TO USE IT

Although most beliefs regarding things done by accident are inauspicious, mistakenly putting underwear on inside out is an exception, and if you happen to do so, wear it like that for the rest of the day for good luck. If you're having a bad day, try turning your underwear inside out, and your day should improve. Wearing red underwear when gambling, flying in a plane, or really any time you need an extra hit of luck is a good idea. Although if it's your wedding day, as some early English superstitions suggest, going commando is a luckier bet.

WISHBONE

WHY IT IS LUCKY

Back before alarm clocks and grocery stores, people relied on the crowing of roosters and hens to tell them when it was daytime and inform them when fresh eggs were available. As a result, these birds got the reputation of being able to tell the future, and hence the origins of the hen oracle. Hen oracle, you ask? Yes, hen oracle. This comes to us courtesy of the Romans (via the Etruscans), who carried the belief along with them when they conquered England. In ancient times, hens were killed and their entrails read by diviners. After the fun was over, the collarbone (the wishbone) was removed and hung out to dry, and the person seeking answers would make a wish on it. Afterward, two lucky observers also got to make wishes, each taking one end of the dried bone and pulling. The person with the larger end, the "lucky break," was the one whose wish would come true. Of course, none of this explains that crazy dancing chicken scene in Werner Herzog's *Stroszek*, but probably nothing can.

HOW TO USE IT

Do as the Romans did: remove the wishbone from a chicken or turkey, clean it off, and hang it to dry. Be sure to keep it out of the reach of small children, cats, and dogs. Once it is dry, enlist a friend, make a wish, and pull!

LUCKY LIVING

Every culture around the world has advice to give when it comes to creating a lucky living space. The Chinese have been working on this for so long (four thousand+ years) that it's become a virtual science (and cottage industry), called "feng shui." In a nutshell, feng shui is the belief that an environment can be enhanced by the proper channeling of chi, or lucky energy. If the chi is flowing, so is the luck. But, like ordering from any Chinese menu, you can't have it all or you'd go into an MSG stupor. So we're taking something from column A, something from column B, and picking some things from takeout menus from other cultures to give you a well-balanced meal. Variety is not only the spice of life, but it's the best way to maximize luck.

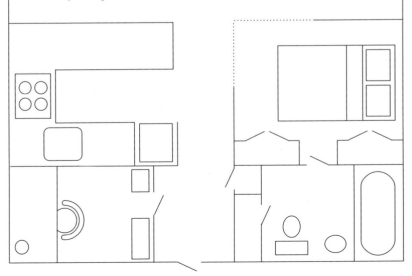

THE FRONT DOOR

*The front door isn't just the place where people come into a home;
it's also where luck (good and bad) makes an entrance.*

....

HOUSE RULES FOR A LUCKY WELCOME

Anyone can tell you that hanging a horseshoe above the doorway
will bring luck. But what if you don't want your home looking like it's
on the set of *Rawhide*? Try hanging a stone with a hole in it near the
door instead. These stones are said to repel the evil eye and any other
free-floating bad luck.

If dangling stones aren't for you, try painting an intricate pattern of
unbroken lines on the threshold. It'll keep bad luck from entering and
allow good luck to thrive.

A house should always be entered through the front door; any other
way could spell trouble. This is especially true for a bride entering her
home for the first time, and to ensure luck, she should be carried over
the threshold.

True adherents to the front-door-only rule won't waver even when
they've forgotten their key. If you must go in through a window (and
we hope you didn't have to break it), once inside you should unlock
the front door, go back out through the window, and then enter
through the front door as originally intended.

When having visitors over, encourage them to enter and leave only by the front door. If they leave through a different door than the one they entered, they could inadvertently walk off with the house's luck.

....

HOME REMEDIES

Slam the door several times when closing it (as they do in central Europe) to trap any bad luck trying to get in between the door and the frame.

Mourners returning from a funeral should enter through a different door than the one they used when leaving the house.

Doors should be opened at the time of childbirth for good luck and to ease delivery. It's also a good assignment to occupy the freaking-out father-to-be.

If you feel as though bad luck has invaded your home and you need a drastic intervention, you can hang the doors the other way around or brick up existing doorways and create new entrances to confuse any agents of misfortune.

THE LIVING ROOM

Long gone are the days of plastic-covered couches, chairs you aren't allowed to sit on, and shag carpets that need to be raked once walked across. Today, the living room has surpassed the other rooms to become the most popular in the house. It's a place to relax, hang out, inadvertently fall asleep, and entertain, so of course it should be designed to be lucky.

....

HOUSE RULES FOR A LUCKY LIVING ROOM

① Everyone should be able to see the entrance to the room from where they are sitting without having to perform any contortions. This promotes a sense of security, which creates an opportunity for good luck. ② If you can't arrange the furniture so that every chair or sofa faces the entrance, just make sure that no seat is placed with its back to the door. ③ Clutter and choked-off spaces do not promote good luck. In feng shui parlance, it blocks the flow of chi. Less is more when it comes to luck, so avoid crowding the living room with too much furniture and, unless the room is small, don't push furniture up against a wall; the luck will travel more freely. ④ The coffee table is more than just a place to put your feet up. It is an important symbol of health and well-being in the home, so keep it clean and clutter free at all times to enhance your luck. ⑤ Neither exercise equipment nor office furniture should ever be put in the living room. They bring inappropriate work energy to a space that should be all about pleasure. ⑥ Ideally, the focal point of your living room should be the fireplace, and the furniture should be arranged around it. We know this may not be readily achieved in every home so we're pitching a nice fireplace/door combo unit to Home Depot. ⑦ Peacock feathers or even images of peacocks are very unlucky in the house. The spying "eye" of the peacock feather casts the evil eye and invades the privacy of the home. ⑧ Fill up a favorite vase with semiprecious stones to bring good luck and harmony to the house. After all, the Chinese word for "vase" is *ping*, which also means "peace."

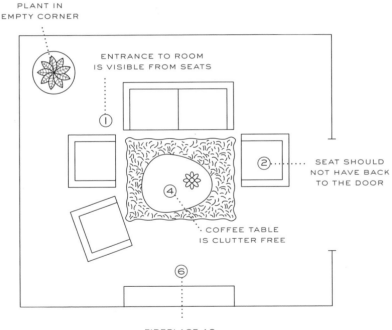

PLANT IN
EMPTY CORNER

ENTRANCE TO ROOM
IS VISIBLE FROM SEATS

SEAT SHOULD
NOT HAVE BACK
TO THE DOOR

COFFEE TABLE
IS CLUTTER FREE

FIREPLACE AS
FOCAL POINT

HOME REMEDIES

Neglected corners and dark areas allow negative energy to pool and fester. Placing lights, mirrors, or plants in these corners will fix that by attracting chi and good luck.

Without being costly, mirrors can double the size of a room and the luck it contains. They can also draw light into a dark corner or reflect the entrance to seating areas where it normally cannot be seen.

Keep your living room walls clear of any violent or sad artwork. You don't have to hang Warhol dollar bills, but the art in your living room should depict symbols of prosperity and harmony.

Flowers and plants in the living room encourage luck, but only if they are *healthy and flourishing*. So black thumbs out there, beware!

If you have the time and inclination, a bright, clean aquarium with healthy live fish (any gold-colored fish is a good option) is particularly efficacious in promoting good fortune at home.

THE FIREPLACE

*From the moment that innovative caveman succeeded in
creating a fire, people have gathered around the hearth. And it's
no wonder that the fireplace remained the center of the home
until that innovative modern man succeeded in creating the
television set. But for luck purposes, it's still all about the fireplace.*

....

HOUSE RULES FOR A LUCKY FIREPLACE

Touch the chimney or mantelpiece for good luck.

Keep any fireplace tools on the right side of the hearth.

....

Hang a bunch of garlic over the fireplace (highly recommended if you believe in vampires).

Place seaweed on your mantelpiece for good luck and to protect your home from fires.

IF YOU'RE PLAYING WITH FIRE DON'T EVER

Use a fireplace for the first time on a Friday.

Allow a fire to go out unintentionally or to burn all night.

....

Point or spit at a fireplace, or spit on logs before building a fire with them.

Build a fire with a friend (it's a surefire way to start an argument).

LUCKY OBJECTS FOR THE HOME

ACORN	An acorn placed on a windowsill will keep lightning out (although it may be unnecessary while you are sleeping, since many believe that lightning will never strike you while you are asleep).
DRAGON	The dragon is a symbol of authority. Placed in a home office it can promote authority and power whether you are the CEO of a Fortune 500 company or just the CEO of your family.
ELEPHANT	Elephants are lucky in many parts of the world, so place an elephant sculpture in the front hall facing inward, or even outside the door, to herald good news and welcome in good luck.
EVERGREEN BRANCH	Nail an evergreen branch to new rafters. This will bring lucky energy to the structure of the house.
HORNET'S NEST	An empty hornet's nest, hung high, is a good-luck charm for the whole family.
HORSE	The horse symbolizes power and movement, so if you like to travel (and who doesn't?), place a horse statue in your home and get your travel luck off to a gallop.

JADE	Prized not just by the Chinese but also by the Mayans and the Maoris, this stone draws prosperity, good health, and luck into your life. It also doubles as a protector, deterring burglars from your home.
LAUGHING BUDDHA	This jolly fellow is a symbol of prosperity, joy, and the proliferation of the family. In Chinese Buddhist homes, he is often prominently placed in the living room, dining room, or family hall.
OLD SHOE	Beginning in medieval Italy, people often wedged an old shoe inside the wall as they constructed a new room. Planting flowers in old boots also ensured good luck in the home. Keep all this in mind before you throw out that old pair of sneakers.
TURTLE	Turtles symbolize longevity and constancy. They can be placed in the rooms of the elderly for luck, but if you ever want to get anything done, they are not recommended for an office or workplace.
UMBRELLA	A closed umbrella symbolizes protection and makes for a lucky security charm if placed near the front entrance of the house.
WINDCHIME	Hang one on your porch or in your backyard to attract good luck.

THE DINING ROOM

For some, the dining room is the primary gathering place for the family. For others, it is a rarely entered space used only on special occasions involving obscenely overstuffed turkeys or late-night poker games. If you're among the second group, remember: neglected spaces are not good for your luck. So even if you don't use your dining room, make sure it's set up properly and well maintained.

....

① Feng shui suggests that the dining room should be on a level equal to or higher than the living room, should never be next to a bathroom or bedroom, and is luckiest when in the center of the house. Keep this in mind if you're lucky enough to design a house from scratch. ② The main feature of any dining room should be the table. To make sure that it's lucky, choose one large enough to accommodate a lot of people, food, and good luck. According the Chinese, squares, rectangles, and octagons are lucky shapes, but round dining tables bring the most luck, since the shape is symbolic of continuity, prosperity, and, perhaps luckiest of all, gold. ③ To maximize luck in the dining room, hang a mirror large enough to reflect the dining table. It will double the food, abundance, wealth, and luck of your family. ④ Put up pictures of decadent foods, ripe fruits, or blossoming flowers to whet everyone's appetite with luck. ⑤ Although some believe that a broken object can only lead to two more breakages, many Russians believe that if a piece of glassware or ceramic breaks at home, it's a sign of good luck. The more valuable the object, the better the luck.

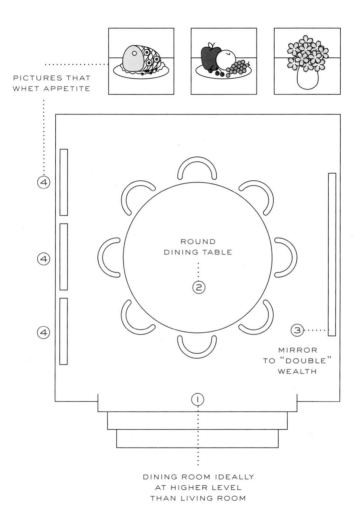

PICTURES THAT
WHET APPETITE

ROUND
DINING TABLE

④

④

④

②

③

MIRROR
TO "DOUBLE"
WEALTH

①

DINING ROOM IDEALLY
AT HIGHER LEVEL
THAN LIVING ROOM

TABLE MANNERS

① PEOPLE Seven guests at the dining table make for a lucky crowd, but thirteen make for—naturally—the worst of luck. Invite an extra neighbor, or call off the party. ② DRINKS For good luck, set drinks down on the table for guests to pick up—don't put a drink directly in a person's hand. ③ BREAD When given the option, tearing bread is infinitely luckier than cutting it, but if cut you must, only do so from one end, please; you'll save yourself a lot of grief. It's bad luck to take the last piece of bread unless it's offered to you, at which point it becomes good luck in either love or money. Whatever you do, don't turn a loaf of bread upside down on a table. ④ CUTLERY It's simple. If you want to keep the peace, keep your silverware uncrossed. Silver forks and knives when laid across one another are magnets for bad luck and quarrels, things to avoid at your nice dinner. And, not that you ever would, but don't ever stir a drink with a knife. It's sure to lead to indigestion, not just for yourself but also for the hostess who is gnashing her teeth while watching you do it. ⑤ CORNERS When assigning seats, save the unlucky corner spot for someone you're not so crazy about. If you were smart enough not to invite people you don't like to dinner, seat a man there over a single woman, since placing a single woman in a corner may do serious damage to her love life. Of course, all this could be avoided with a round dining table. ⑥ NAPKINS Don't fold your napkin at the end of the meal—it's a sign that you'll never return to eat in that household. ⑦ DISHES Food should be passed around the table in a clockwise direction for luck.

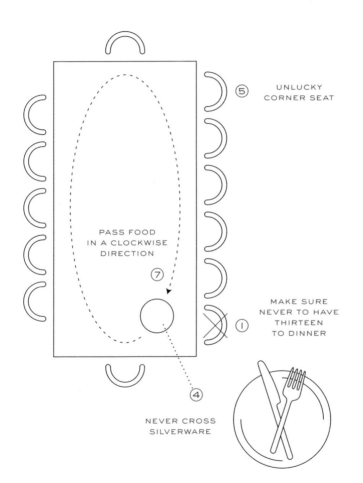

UNLUCKY
CORNER SEAT

PASS FOOD
IN A CLOCKWISE
DIRECTION

MAKE SURE
NEVER TO HAVE
THIRTEEN
TO DINNER

NEVER CROSS
SILVERWARE

THE KITCHEN

Many cultures consider the kitchen the lucky engine of the home.
And it makes sense, if you think about it. Food is symbolic
of health and wealth, and when the luck and money are flowing,
you can afford to eat good food. And good food leads
to good health. And the kitchen is where this all happens.

....

The stove is the centerpiece of the kitchen, and it should always be kept clean and working well for good luck to flow. The burners on the stove represent the wealth-generating potential of your home, so be sure to rotate the usage of your burners on a regular basis; that way the entire stove can be an active, healthy luck producer.

Whoever does the cooking is fundamentally linked to generating the luck of the kitchen. Make sure the cook is able to see the doorway of the kitchen while cooking; hang a mirror above the stove, if necessary, so the cook can always see who is coming and going.

When there's less clutter on your countertops, it frees up more space in the kitchen for food to be prepared and displayed. And it goes without saying, the more food you prepare in the kitchen, the more abundance and good luck you'll have.

Should any of the following events occur in the kitchen, good luck is on the way: bubbles appearing in a cup of coffee, tea leaves floating to the top of a teacup, rice forming a ring around the edge of a pot, a sugar bowl being accidentally knocked over.

KITCHEN LUCK

Keeping a rooster in the kitchen will boost good luck and prosperity. If you can't stomach the thought of having one peck away at you while you're making coq au vin, how about a rooster-shaped casserole dish or rooster pot holders?

Knives should be kept out of sight in a drawer when they aren't being used. They symbolize accidents and violence, so having them lying around visible in the kitchen is unlucky.

Plants in the kitchen help to provide healthy good-luck chi and cleanse the kitchen air.

After baking, it's unlucky for scraps of uncooked dough or pastry to be left over or thrown away. Instead, any remaining scraps should be baked into small lucky treats for children.

A kitchen should never be empty of salt. To ensure good luck, keep at least one small sachet of salt tucked away at the back of your pantry at all times.

Jewish superstition dictates that something should always be left in the oven, since empty ovens mean that the cook will lack the food to cook in it. But since leaving any food in the oven invites all sorts of unwelcome creatures, leaving a baking tray or some other utensil in the oven will suffice.

THE BEDROOM

HOW LUCKY IS YOUR BED?

You likely spend more time in your bed than anywhere else at home, so this piece of furniture and how you position it is central to all the luck in your house.

....

First off, you need to make sure the bed is placed in the luckiest spot in the room. To determine where that is exactly, follow these guidelines: (1) To ensure that no bad-luck lines cross you while you sleep, place your bed in line with any floorboards and ceiling beams rather than across them. (2) Make sure you can see the door from where you sleep. (3) The bed is also luckiest when placed diagonally to the door, and as far away from it as possible. This was probably learned the hard way by the unlucky caveman who decided to sleep at the mouth of the cave. (4) Note where the windows are located, and avoid sleeping with your head close to one. Smart people don't want their luck to "fly out the window" while they sleep. If you can't help but sleep under a window, put up heavy drapes to stop the luck from escaping. (5) Having lots of lucky energy actively flowing around you is normally a good thing, but maybe not so much when you're trying to sleep. Chi tends to travel between the door and any windows, so unless you want to be caught up in a constant wind tunnel while you sleep, don't position your bed in this draft. (6) Pay attention to what is under your bed, not just because you've seen too many repeats of *Friday the 13th* on late-night cable, but also because dust bunnies and clutter under the bed will detract from your good luck. ⑦ If you sleep with another person, note the position of your bed relative to the nearest wall. A shared bed crammed into the corner of a room gives one partner more freedom, while the other will literally and symbolically feel up against a wall. For optimal luck in the relationship, place the bed so there is equal space on either side. ⑧ Matching bedside tables give added stability and protection, which is good for your luck (and your relationship). Something to keep in mind with bedroom furniture is that you don't want any sharp corners (and their negative, unlucky energy) pointing toward the bed. ⑨ Always make the bed in one go, or risk your day not going smoothly. ⑩ It's unlucky for more than three people to share a bed, although if you're one of them, you may know more about luck than we do.

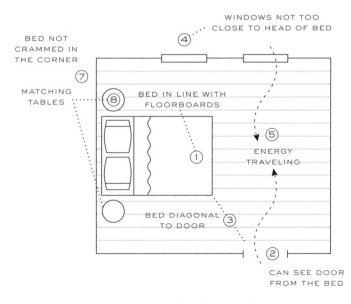

WINDOWS NOT TOO
CLOSE TO HEAD OF BED

BED NOT
CRAMMED IN
THE CORNER

④

⑦

MATCHING
TABLES

⑧

BED IN LINE WITH
FLOORBOARDS

⑤

ENERGY
TRAVELING

①

BED DIAGONAL
TO DOOR

③

②

CAN SEE DOOR
FROM THE BED

SWEET DREAMS

Hang a piece of coral over the bed. This lucky object from the sea, worn for centuries by the Chinese to prevent insanity, is believed to ward off nightmares and bring good luck while you sleep.

WHICH SIDE, PLEASE?

Although "getting up on the wrong side of the bed" is a familiar phrase (and experience), there seems to be no clear consensus on exactly which side is actually the luckier one. Some believe that it's unlucky to get out of bed on a different side than the one you got in on, while others think that the opposite is true. Traditionalists are convinced that one should always get up from the right side of the bed, since the left is the "devil's side" (he sat on the left side of God's throne back in the days when he was still in favor up there). In the absence of clear guidelines, you're just going to have to pay close attention to determine which side works better for you, and then stick with it as your lucky side. And, since many of those living in small urban apartments have no choice as to which side they get up on, simply be sure to put your right sock, stocking, or shoe on first when dressing in the morning as an antidote to any potential bad luck.

LUCK ON THE WALLS

The images you surround yourself with in the
bedroom can have a powerful effect on the
luck in your life. Remove any images that represent
conflict, solitude, aggression, or hard work. Hang
something that makes you feel happy or motivated.
This includes a velvet Elvis if it works for you.

To bring luck in romance into the bedroom,
place images that will put you in a romantic
mood in these two key places: the wall
opposite the foot of the bed (where you naturally
look when lying down), and whatever area
of the room you first see when you enter.

Hang your pictures perfectly horizontal
to the floor for the best of luck, and never put
a picture above a door or over the bed.

....

HOME REMEDIES

If you have a bathroom, toilet, or shower leading off of your bedroom, make sure that the toilet seat is down and the door is always shut to be sure good luck isn't flushed away.

Anything placed in pairs (candles, decorative pillows, knickknacks) is good luck for your love life.

Although it may work in the Playboy mansion, avoid sleeping with your image visible in a mirror or having a mirror at the head or foot of your bed.

Soft lighting is ideal, so avoid hanging harsh ceiling lamps directly over your bed.

Make sure all the lights in the bedroom are working, replace any burned-out bulbs, and be alert for dark corners where you need to increase the lucky energy by adding more light.

Plants and flowers, while lucky in the living room, are better left out of the bedroom.

Don't exercise or store sporting equipment in the bedroom unless you enjoy relationships that feel like tough workouts.

Make sure your bedroom door opens easily and completely. Doors that stick, squeak, or only open partway because of all the stuff stored behind them block romantic luck. A loose doorknob could also mean you're having a hard time getting a handle on romance.

GOOD HOUSEKEEPING

Do your spring-cleaning before the month of June. This lucky tradition takes its cue from the Jewish custom of having the house ready in time for Passover.

Brooms, mops, and any other cleaning equipment should be hidden away when not in use, as leaving them out can symbolically sweep away good luck or, if left in the dining room, all your food.

Sweep in good luck the Mayan way by cleaning the doorways and stairs of your home with a broom that's been dunked in basil water. Simply fill a bucket with hot water and basil leaves, dip, and then start sweeping. This good-luck custom works best if repeated for nine days in a row, beginning on a Thursday or Friday.

Sheets in a guest room should never be changed until the guest has left your house for more than an hour, and sheets should never be turned down early in the day, or bad luck may make itself comfy there.

LUCK IN THE GARDEN

Even the greenest of green thumbs knows that plenty of good luck is required when trying to make a garden grow and that a run of bad luck can undermine the best intentions.

....

For healthy roses, throw a dead fish in the bottom of the planting hole.

Place a few tourmalines in the soil around your plants. This crystal is known to be good luck for greenery and also keeps insects away from the plants.

To make sure a mango tree bears fruit, drive a nail into the mango when planting it.

Scatter rusty nails or old irons around your plants to give them a lucky boost.

Put a piece of palm branch from Palm Sunday in the hole you've dug when planting any tree or shrub.

Have a pregnant woman help you in the garden; expectant women lend luck to anything they plant.

Buy a garden gnome. Their name is derived from the Ancient Germanic word *Kuba-Walda*, which means "home administrator" or "home spirit." And not only are they kitschy and fun, they'll bring good luck to your outdoor endeavors.

LUNAR GARDENING

The leading lucky charm for all things green is the moon, so look up at the sky and pay attention to the phase of the moon before you do any planting to ensure your plants get off to a lucky start.

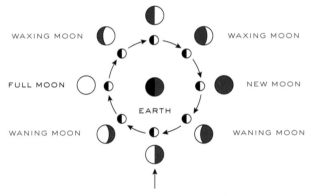

WAXING MOON

WAXING MOON

FULL MOON

NEW MOON

EARTH

WANING MOON

WANING MOON

VIEW OF THE MOON FROM EARTH

Flowers will bloom best if planted during the time of a new moon.

Rooting plants that grow below the ground (carrots, tubers, etc.) are best planted on a waning moon.

Everything else that grows above the ground (shrubs, trees, etc.) should be planted on a waxing moon.

LUCKY PLANTS

*It's nice to have plants around the house, so why not choose lucky
ones while you're at it? The healthier and more vibrant your plants,
the luckier they are. Succulent plants are especially lucky because they
are thought to be ripe and bursting with good fortune. Needless to say,
dry or dead leaves should be removed immediately. Here are some
plants that are lucky inside, outside, or anywhere around the house.*

ALOE	Hang over the doorway, as they do in Africa, to offer good luck and to prevent accidents.
BAMBOO	The Chinese believe this lucky plant brings prosperity, health, and longevity.
CACTUS	The thorns ward off the evil eye, and no home should be without one near the entrance.
HOUSELEEK	Plant on the roof as a lucky guardian against lightning strikes and fire.
JADE PLANT	Shopkeepers in Asia keep this plant around to increase their luck in business.
MONEY PLANT	Extremely popular as a good-luck gift during the Chinese New Year, it's especially lucky if you find one with seven leaves on a single stem.

LUCKY TREES

Besides bolstering property prices, offering shade, and attracting the random stray cat, trees can bring good luck to the house and its occupants.

CHERRY TREE	A great place to meet a future lover, the tree offers good luck in romance.
COTTONWOOD TREE	The "sacred rustling tree" of the Sioux Indians, only its wood is lucky enough to be used as the centerpiece in their sacred lodges.
HAWTHORN	Will defend the house against bad luck when planted nearby.
LEMON TREE	Plant one near the front of your home as a powerful good-luck charm. It's luckier still when full of fruit.
LIME TREE	Plant this bad-luck sponge near the front door to absorb bad luck before it can get inside.
OAK TREE	The mighty oak is mighty lucky—just ask any Druid you know.
ROWAN	Revered since Celtic times, this ancient tree offers good luck anywhere it's planted.

FLOWER POWER

Flowers can impress a date or cheer up a friend,
but did you know that certain blossoms are lucky when they
are planted in the garden or brought into the house?

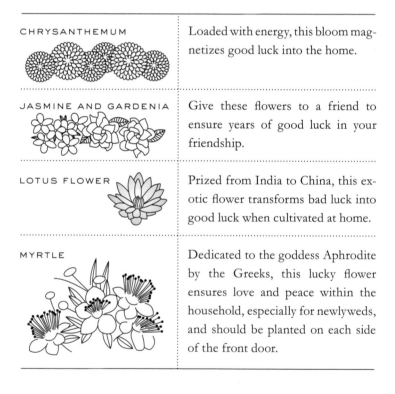

CHRYSANTHEMUM	Loaded with energy, this bloom magnetizes good luck into the home.
JASMINE AND GARDENIA	Give these flowers to a friend to ensure years of good luck in your friendship.
LOTUS FLOWER	Prized from India to China, this exotic flower transforms bad luck into good luck when cultivated at home.
MYRTLE	Dedicated to the goddess Aphrodite by the Greeks, this lucky flower ensures love and peace within the household, especially for newlyweds, and should be planted on each side of the front door.

NARCISSUS 	This bloom brings booming business—cross your fingers that it blooms within the first fifteen days of the New Year for good fortune.
NIGHT-BLOOMING CEREUS	This rare flower blooms so infrequently, sometimes only once in a decade, that it is considered to be the height of good fortune in Asia if you ever witness it. The blooming process lasts but a few hours and fills the air with an intoxicating perfume.
PEACH BLOSSOM	Hang a sprig over the front door to keep bad luck at bay.
PEONY	This flower is a good choice for a date if it's someone you're serious about, since it's known for bringing powerful good luck in romance.
SUNFLOWER	As this heliotrope follows the path of the sun, it also beams good luck around the whole garden.

BETTER LEFT OUTSIDE

Unless you're convinced otherwise, a good rule of thumb for flowers is that if they are white, it's generally not a good idea to bring them into the house. Associated with funerals and death across many cultures for centuries, the color white is often believed to be a harbinger of bad luck. Such unlucky flowers include daffodils, white lilacs, primroses, and snowdrops. It's also best to avoid bringing in dried flowers or any flowers that have bloomed out of season. White or not, the following flowers are best left in the garden.

CHERRY BLOSSOM

Although the tree itself is lucky outside the house, cherry blossoms picked in the spring will bring you bad luck all through the summer.

HAWTHORN

Simply put, the hawthorn smells like death. The scent of this quickly decaying flower developed a bad reputation in the seventeenth century, supposedly reminding the English of the odor of decaying bodies during the Great Plague.

HONEYSUCKLE

Straightlaced Victorians believed that bringing this flower's scent into the house would cause a daughter to bloom too quickly—bad luck for fathers who thought even table legs were too sexy to be exposed.

HYDRANGEA

Those same Victorians believed the exact opposite fate would befall a daughter if hydrangeas were allowed in the house—bad luck for fathers who didn't want to support spinster daughters forever.

LILY OF THE VALLEY

Thought to represent "the tears of the virgin," lilies of the valley brought inside, or even planted in your garden, will bring bad luck.

WHAT ABOUT THOSE CHRISTMAS PLANTS?

Holly, ivy, and mistletoe are classic Christmas decorations, but few realize that their origins as good-luck charms date back centuries before men began donning red velvet suits with padding and making kids cry.

HOLLY 	The Romans gave holly as a gift of good luck during their midwinter festivals, and in the Middle Ages it was popularly planted under windowsills, in the belief that it would repel witches. Witches supposedly hated holly even more than they hated eating skinny children.
IVY 	Ivy was dedicated to Bacchus, the Roman god of wine, and since the times of Pax Romana, the plant has been hung outside taverns, inns, and pubs to indicate that alcoholic beverages are sold inside. If it grew naturally on the walls of houses, it was said to bring good luck to all those inside, but if the plant started to decay, it was a sure sign of misfortune for the household.

MISTLETOE

Although these days it is largely associated with kissing opportunities, mistletoe was a sacred plant of the ancient Druids, who harvested it with golden sickles and never allowed it to touch the ground, which is perhaps why, to this day, it's always found hanging. The Druids hung the lucky plant over doorways and in the center of rooms to protect and cure all those who passed under it. In fact, the Roman historian Pliny records that the Druidic name for *mistletoe* meant "heal all."

HOW TO USE THEM

Bring holly and ivy into the house for good luck only on Christmas Eve, and remove it from the house by Twelfth Night (January 5) to avoid the luck turning bad.

Keep mistletoe hanging throughout the year for good luck, and replace with a new sprig every Christmas Eve. Mistletoe should also only be cut during the Christmas season.

Hang mistletoe in the most highly trafficked area of your house so that its luck will rub off constantly on all who pass under it. Kissing is optional.

LUCKY CREATURES FROM THE GARDEN

BEE	If a bee flies into the house, it's a sign that luck may be buzzing your way.
BUTTERFLY	Butterflies are lovely and may seem like symbols of good luck, but it gets a little more complicated than that. Seeing one white butterfly is lucky, but seeing one yellow butterfly means that you may be getting sick soon. And then seeing any three together on a single leaf, unlikely as it sounds, is surely a sign of bad luck.
CATERPILLAR	Don't freak out if a caterpillar wriggles onto you in the garden—just follow the custom and toss it over your left shoulder for a quick dose of good luck. The same can be done with an equally lucky—but more slimy—snail.

CRICKET	Crickets are lucky creatures to have in your garden and you should never harm them. If one finds its way into your kitchen, it's a sign of good luck. Their singing is believed to work a charm that keeps bad luck away at night.
LADYBUG	Ladybugs are good luck if you find them in your garden. Even luckier is if one happens to land on you, but only if you don't brush her off. Count the number of spots on her back, since it's believed that each spot represents a lucky month for you. Send her away with the rhyme "Ladybug, ladybug, fly away home; your house is on fire and your children are gone."
PRAYING MANTIS	Seeing a praying mantis in the garden is considered good luck. In Asia, they are so revered that Shaolin monks even developed a fighting style based on their movements.

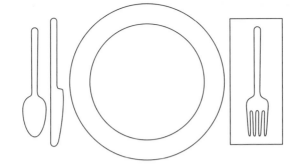

POTLUCK

You are what you eat, so why not eat, drink, and be lucky? The recipes that follow include fortunate foods to eat for many of life's important events and are accompanied by tips for drinking and dining with luck, international advice on what to eat at New Year's to ensure a lucky year ahead, and a guide to ingredients that will help spice up your food with good fortune. Be prepared to turn *Bon appétit* into *Bonne chance*!

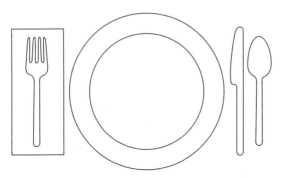

CHEERS TO LUCK

The tradition of raising a glass and drinking to someone's health has its origins in a practical purpose—it was intended to assure guests that the drinks being offered were not poisoned. As far back as ancient Greece, a host would pour and take a drink from a common decanter and then invite his guests to do likewise, giving his pledge of their shared good health. When being poisoned by a host became a less pressing concern, glasses were simply clinked together in health and in the belief that the noise would ward off any evil spirits lurking about. The use of the word *toast* appears to be almost as old, and stems from the incomprehensible-today-but-apparently-fairly-common practice of putting a piece of toast into a glass of wine or ale to improve the drink's taste. Skip the charred bread, but remember these lucky guidelines anytime you make a toast.

....

If you're pouring the wine, make sure it's with your right hand. And if you're going to pass the wine bottle, always send it off in a clockwise direction.

If you're not drinking any alcohol, it's luckiest if you add a drop of wine to whatever you're drinking before clinking.

Never toast with water—it is preferable to raise an empty glass. If your glass is filled with water, be sure not to touch glasses with anyone else, as it invites bad luck.

Always make and maintain eye contact with each person as you touch each other's glasses.

If you spill a bit of wine while toasting, don't worry about it. It may be slightly embarrassing, but it's a sign of good luck.

Don't stand or raise your glass if you are the subject of a toast. It's like clapping for yourself and considered bad luck, not to mention bad manners.

After the toast, be sure to take a sip before resting the glass on the table.

BUBBLY LUCK

Legend has it that champagne, the quintessential good-luck beverage, was invented by accident when some monks put a stopper made out of cork, instead of the usual leaky flax, into a bottle. The story goes that the Church believed the resulting effervescence was the work of evil spirits and banned the drink's manufacture. When the French kings took a liking to the drink, the Church's ban fizzled out. In reality, champagne was perfected over many centuries by vintners experimenting with the fermentation process to create the carbon dioxide bubbles. And it has been used the world over to celebrate the beginning of a fortuitous event—from childbirth to marriage to the sealing of a business deal. Starting in the nineteenth century, champagne bottles were smashed against the side of a ship before its maiden voyage. This ritual harkens back to early seafaring days when a human or animal sacrifice was made to appease the sea gods. In more modern times, wine became the substitute for blood.

LUCK, SHAKEN, NOT STIRRED

Get lucked up!

FRIAR'S LUCK

In medieval times it was customary for a friar to invite himself to
your meal to share his sacrament and bring good luck to your home.
Since friars don't seem to get out much these days, you can have
a lucky drink in their honor instead.

1 oz. dark rum

1 oz. lemon juice

2 oz. Frangelico

1 tsp. Grenadine

1 orange slice

Mix the dark rum, juice, Frangelico, and Grenadine in a shaker
with cracked ice. Pour into an old-fashioned glass and garnish
with the orange slice.

These cocktails may not have the pedigree of a friar's blessing, but with the right bartender's alchemy, they can still bestow a fair bit of luck.

LUCKY DOUBLE

½ lemon, cut into quarters

½ oz. orange liqueur

2 oz. vodka

Drop the lemon pieces into a mixing glass. Pour in the orange liqueur and muddle well. Add the vodka and some ice, shake well, and pour into a tall glass.

LUCKY SEVEN

½ oz. vodka	½ oz. peach liqueur
½ oz. whiskey	½ oz. sloe gin
½ oz. amaretto	1 splash cranberry juice
½ oz. orange liqueur	1 splash orange juice
½ oz. Cuban rum	1 splash lime juice

Pour the seven liquors, straight, into a tall glass. Top with a splash each of cranberry, orange, and lime juices. Serve in a collins glass.

LUCKY HERBS AND SPICES

See your spice rack in a whole new light.

ALFALFA	This lucky herb is thought to enhance the fortune of all those who carry it, particularly gamblers.
ALLSPICE	Allspice is the dried fruit of the *Pimenta dioica* plant, said to attract luck to business ventures. Sprinkle it in the four corners of your workplace.
BASIL	Basil is the essential good-luck herb for every home. Place crushed basil in one corner of every room, or soak basil leaves in water for three days and then sprinkle that— albeit soggy—mixture around.
CHAMOMILE	Who knew that this soothing tea popular with insomniacs could also enhance your romantic luck? It's also lucky for gamblers when they wash their hands in it. Casino bathroom attendants, take note.
CINNAMON	Known for its protective qualities, cinnamon has been used since ancient times for defense and to enhance prosperity. Sprinkle some in your wallet when you need a confidence booster or to bolster communication skills.

GALANGAL	This staple of Southeast Asian cuisine is thought to promote luck and prosperity. Its sword-shaped leaves may also have something to do with the herb's supposed powers of protection.
JUNIPER BERRIES	Found in Egyptian tombs and prized by ancient Greeks for increasing stamina during the Olympic games, the juniper berry is believed to enhance financial success *and* luck in the bedroom.
NUTMEG	Once one of the world's most valuable commodities, nutmeg today can be used as a good-luck charm to increase the size of one's gambling winnings.
STAR ANISE 	Revered in Japan for its lucky properties, the seeds and bark of this evergreen tree are used as incense in temples, where the tree itself is commonly planted on the grounds (and also in cemeteries) for luck.

THE LUCKIEST HERB
GARLIC

Long before the vampire-slaying industry began to promote it as the ultimate protector against creatures of the night, garlic was already a symbol of good luck in almost every country that cultivated it. And even before its considerable medicinal qualities were proven through scientific study, it was known as a good-luck charm for curing illness. The ancient Egyptians believed garlic to be a gift from the gods, even going so far as worshipping the bulbs as deities, while the Romans boosted their courage by eating cloves of garlic before going into battle. To this day, some matadors in Spain still carry garlic into the bull-ring, believing that it will protect them from charging *toros*. Bunches of garlic were hung on the mantel or as wreaths over doorways in homes from Greece to Ireland, and sometimes even rubbed on cooking utensils to ward off bad luck. And, of course, to protect against debonair bloodsuckers with strange accents, it was always considered advisable to wear a necklace made out of garlic bulbs around your neck when you went to bed. As for trying to get a kiss after eating it—well, good luck.

THE UNLUCKIEST HERB
PARSLEY

The next time you think about garnishing a dish with some sprigs of parsley, you might want to think again. The ancient Greeks regarded parsley as the sacred herb of the dead, and the Romans used it to decorate their graves, so, not surprisingly, it's become infused with unlucky connotations. Plutarch, the first-century Roman historian, tells the story of a battle between the Greek army and a much smaller Celtic force. The crafty Celtic leader blanketed a hundred donkeys with parsley and sent them out to greet the advancing Greek troops, who fled in horror at the sight of the dreaded plant. It was believed that only wicked people could grow the "devil's herb" well—perhaps, on a note of realism, because of the notoriously long germination period that the herb has to endure (it was said that the seeds had to go "to hell and back" before sprouting). It is also unlucky to give parsley away or to replant it—moving it from an old home to a new one would simply transplant all the bad luck of the past to the new home.

LUCKY RECIPES

CHINESE BIRTHDAY NOODLES
WITH CHICKEN AND SHRIMP

In China and other Asian countries, it's practically required by law to eat noodles on your birthday, because the long noodles represent long life. You can find Chinese-style noodles in the refrigerator section of your grocery store. The noodles should not be snapped in half before boiling or cut while eating, since short noodles not only defeat the purpose but may even bring bad luck. This recipe combines lucky longevity noodles with eggs, another symbol of good luck and abundance to the Chinese.

CHINESE BIRTHDAY NOODLES

¼ lb. snow peas	½ tsp. white pepper
1 bunch broccoli florets	¼ cup cornstarch
2 medium carrots, sliced	5 tbsp. olive oil
½ lb. medium-size shrimp,	1 clove garlic, chopped fine
shelled and deveined	1 cup canned chicken broth
4 large eggs	1 tbsp. sesame oil
1 lb. Chinese-style noodles	Soy sauce to taste
½ lb. chicken-breast meat	Salt and white pepper to taste
2 tsp. salt	1 spring onion, chopped

Boil all the vegetables and shrimp separately until just cooked. Drain and set aside. Beat the eggs, fry into an omelet, and shred into thin slices. Scald the Chinese noodles in hot water and rinse quickly in cold water.

Cut chicken into strips and coat well with salt, pepper, and cornstarch. In a large frying pan, heat the olive oil, and cook the garlic until lightly browned. Add the chicken to the pan and sauté until cooked. Next, add the shrimp, then add the vegetables, and then the noodles. Stir in the chicken broth and combine well, adding soy sauce, sesame oil, salt, and pepper to taste. Place on a serving plate and garnish with the shredded omelet. Sprinkle chopped spring onions and serve immediately.

Serves six.

....

GNOCCHI DELLA FORTUNA
(Gnocchi with Butter and Sage)

Don't let the Italian-sounding name fool you—this dish actually hails from Brazil. The story goes that a very poor man passed through a small village on the twenty-ninth day of the month in search of a meal. A kindly old couple offered the man the only food they had on the table that day, gnocchi, which he ate with much gratitude. Some time later, the man returned to the village with the news that his luck had changed tremendously since the day he had eaten the couple's gnocchi, and he had made a great fortune. Since then, Brazilians have eaten *gnocchi della fortuna* in the hopes of devouring that same good luck. The custom works with any type of gnocchi and sauce, and we've provided the classic butter and sage recipe. Here's how the lucky part works.

① Wait until the twenty-ninth day of the month.

② Place a dollar bill (or any amount you wish, as long as it's a paper bill) underneath the plate of gnocchi before eating it.

③ Eat the first seven gnocchi while standing up.

④ Keep the money that you had placed under your plate for thirty days, and then donate it to a needy person. Your act of generosity will return as good luck to you.

GNOCCHI DELLA FORTUNA

2 lb. potatoes, peeled	Salt to taste
1 cup flour, *plus more as needed*	5 tbsp. butter
1 egg	6 fresh sage leaves
Milk as needed	Nutmeg to taste
Bread crumbs as needed	Parmesan cheese

Gnocchi:

Boil the potatoes until they are cooked through. Mash them while they are still warm. Slowly add the flour and then the egg, mixing until the dough is soft and elastic. If the dough feels too dry, add a bit of milk. If it feels too wet, add some bread crumbs or more flour. Roll the dough out in long snakelike forms about 1 inch in diameter. Cut into pieces roughly 1 inch long. Flour the outsides lightly so they don't stick, and place them on a napkin. Boil the gnocchi in a pot of salted water, being careful that they don't stick together as they cook. When the gnocchi float to the top of the water, they are done (they should cook for at least 5 minutes). Take them out of the pot with a slotted wooden spoon, and put them in a bowl. Top immediately with the butter-sage sauce. Sprinkle nutmeg on top. Serve with freshly grated Parmesan cheese.

Butter and Sage Sauce:

In a shallow pan, melt the butter and add the sage so that it cooks lightly, flavoring the butter (about 3 to 5 minutes). *Serves six.*

LUCKY FOODS FOR THE NEW YEAR

It seems like no matter what time zone you live in, New Year's marks an opportunity to usher in good luck via the dining table. Some people begin eating the moment the clock strikes twelve, while others have already enjoyed their New Year's Eve feasts or are preparing for one the next day. Here are some of the lucky gastronomical New Year's traditions from around the globe.

....

AUSTRIA

It's all about the lucky pig in Austria for New Year's, where everything from suckling pig to little pigs made out of marzipan is traditionally served. The pigs symbolize a plentiful future and good eating, because, let's face it, any family that owns a pig is bound to eat well.

BRAZIL

At midnight on New Year's Eve, Brazilians up and down the coast head for the sea and jump through seven waves. When they return, the first meal of the brand-new year is always lentils and rice, since the coinlike shape of the lentil signifies wealth.

FRANCE

The French celebrate New Year's Eve with a feast called Le Réveillon de la Saint-Sylvestre. This special dinner is believed to bring prosperity to the house, and customary dishes include crêpes, foie gras, and, of course, lots of champagne. During Candlemas, on February 2, at the Fête de la Chandeleur, more crepes are consumed. A gold coin should be held in the left hand while flipping the crepe with the right hand to ensure good luck and riches for the entire year.

LATIN COUNTRIES

From Spain to Venezuela, people can be found eating twelve grapes at the stroke of midnight (although Peruvians go one step further and eat thirteen). Eaten one by one, each grape symbolizes a month in the coming year. The sweetest grape corresponds to your luckiest month, while the most sour tells you which month to look out for.

THE NETHERLANDS

The word *Oliebollen*, translated literally as "oil balls," may not sound particularly appetizing, but these delicious deep-fried sweet donuts filled with raisins, apples, or currants are devoured by the Dutch on New Year's Eve. The tradition dates back to the myth of the Germanic goddess Perchta, who would fly through the midwinter sky and attempt to cut open the bellies of anyone she came across. The fat from the Oliebollen would protect those who ate them, as Perchta's sword would slide off their bodies without harm.

THE PHILIPPINES

Sometimes, it's not really about the food, but more about the table. Filipinos believe that come midnight on New Year's Eve, every dining table should be groaning to the edges with numerous plates of food. This ensures continued abundance in the coming year.

SICILY

The cardinal rule for the New Year's meal in Sicily is this: good luck comes only to those who eat lasagna. Those who eat fettuccine, macaroni, fusilli, tagliatelle, or any other pasta do so at their own risk.

SINGAPORE

Yusheng is a raw fish salad invented fifteen hundred years ago in the southern Chinese coastal areas but popularized by enterprising Singaporean chefs in the 1960s. The name in Mandarin translates to "raw fish," but the words also sound like "good luck rising." To literally witness their good luck rise, families and friends gather around the dining table on the seventh night of the Chinese New Year and toss the shredded ingredients of the dish in the air with chopsticks while making auspicious wishes for the coming year.

SWITZERLAND

Cream symbolizes wealth, so the Swiss believe that an abundance of wealth and good luck will come by dropping dollops of cream on the floor on New Year's Day. It kind of makes you wonder whose lucky job it is to clean up the mess.

AND THEN THERE'S CHINA

In a culture where food and symbolism are paramount, eating for good luck is the main event during the Chinese New Year. Families traditionally gather on the Lunar New Year's Eve for a sumptuous banquet, where certain foods take on a special lucky meaning and dishes are served for their significance of name or appearance. Dumplings are a favorite because their shape resembles the gold nugget. The sweet and sticky glutinous New Year's rice cake Nian Gao is eaten to promote a higher standard of living, because the Chinese word *nian*, meaning "sticky," also means "year," while the word *gao*, or "cake," also means "high." Mandarin oranges are passed out to everyone, since these vibrantly colored fruits not only symbolize good fortune, but the word itself, *kum*, or "orange," sounds like "gold" in Cantonese. Fish figures prominently during the banquet, since the word for "fish," *yu*, sounds like both the word meaning "abundance" and the word meaning "wish." As a result, families traditionally eat a whole fish to symbolize the wish for abundance in the coming year.

HOPPIN' JOHN AND COLLARD GREENS

In the American South, eating hoppin' John and collards on New Year's Day is believed to bring good luck and wealth in the upcoming year. Although no one is sure of the origin of the name, everyone seems to agree that eating the dish will bring good fortune. The black-eyed peas symbolize coins, the rice abundance, and the collards, flat and green, dollar bills. Some people even throw a real coin into the mix during preparation. The diner who finds it in their dish will be the recipient of an extra helping of good luck. Fill your plate, and your bank account will follow!

HOPPIN' JOHN

1 lb. dried black-eyed peas	1 medium yellow onion,
soaked overnight, or two	peeled and diced
15 oz. cans	1 tsp. crushed red-
1 ham hock, or ½ lb. cubed	pepper flakes
ham or smoked sausage	Salt and pepper to taste
2 stalks celery, chopped	Tabasco to taste

Place all ingredients in a heavy-bottomed pot, adding several dashes of Tabasco (to taste). Cover with water, bring to a boil, and then simmer, covered, for 35 to 40 minutes, until peas are tender. Serve in bowls over white rice, adding extra Tabasco or pepper sauce to taste. *Serves eight.*

COLLARD GREENS

Collards (two or three large bunches)	Olive oil (optional)
	1 tbsp. vinegar
1 ham hock (optional)	Tabasco to taste
3 cloves garlic	Salt and pepper to taste
½ tsp. crushed red-pepper flakes	

Wash collards in several changes of cold water, making sure to remove all grit. Trim large stems to the leaf level. In small batches, roll leaves together and cut once lengthwise through the center, and then cut crosswise into 2-inch strips.

Place ham hock in heavy-bottomed pot and cover with water. Bring water to a boil and then simmer hock for 30 minutes before adding collards, garlic, and pepper flakes; or, for vegetarian option, add olive oil to the pot and heat, sauté garlic and pepper flakes, then greens, for a few minutes before covering with cold water. Cover, bring to a boil, and simmer over low heat for an hour, until tender. Season with the vinegar, a few good shakes of Tabasco, and salt and pepper as necessary. *Serves eight.*

VASILOPITA

Vasilopita, also known as St. Basil's cake, is a sweet cake that is baked at New Year's in Greek households to bless the house and welcome good fortune. This age-old custom dates back to the fourth century, when St. Basil sought to secretly distribute money to the poor. He devised a plan to have gold coins hidden in cakes and made sure that they found their way to the neediest families in his diocese. In this way, the families were able to enjoy the cake, along with the bonus of coming into some unexpected scratch, without feeling like it was charity. Today, the dessert should be served with the whole family gathered around the table. As each piece is sliced, the name of the recipient should be said aloud. The very first piece is always cut in either the name of St. Basil or in the name of the house in which the cake was baked. Slices are then served, beginning with the most senior member of the house and ending with the youngest, and whoever gets the coin is considered especially lucky for the year. The first slice cut for the house is eaten last, and if the coin is found there, then your home will have all the luck!

VASILOPITA

4 eggs (whole)	Pinch of salt
3 egg yolks	Zest of 1 whole orange
2 cups sugar	4 tbsp. fresh orange juice
1 lb. butter (room temp.)	½ tsp. vanilla extract
3 to 4 cups flour	2 cups finely ground almonds
3 tsp. baking powder	Powdered sugar and other
½ tsp. baking soda	decorations

Preheat oven to 350°F. Find a shiny coin (any currency will do). Wash and wrap in tinfoil. Set aside. Beat eggs, egg yolks, and sugar until fluffy. Add butter and mix until creamy. In a separate bowl, mix 3 cups flour with baking powder, baking soda, salt, and orange zest. Add this to the egg/butter mixture and blend. Pour in orange juice and vanilla and mix well.

Fold in almonds. If mixture is too watery at this point, slowly add up to 1 more cup of flour. The consistency should be like really thick (but not sticky) pancake batter. Pour into either two 8-inch greased baking forms or one 10-inch form, and drop in lucky coin. Be sure to fill the pan only halfway, as the cake will rise. Bake for 60 to 75 minutes, depending on the size of the baking pan. Let cake cool completely. Sprinkle with powdered sugar. Using almond slivers, chocolate chips, stencils, or any other cake decorations, write the numbers of the incoming year (e.g., "2010") across the center of the cake. *Serves eight to ten.*

 (UN)LUCKY SPILLS

WINE If the toasting gets too lively, don't fret if you spill a little wine. Wine spilled on the floor is considered to be a lucky tribute to your ancestors, and wine spilled on the table is a lucky symbol of sharing among good company.

MILK There's no way around it; you're in for seven days of bad luck. Just consider yourself fortunate that it's milk and not a mirror.

BREAD If you make a wish when you pick up dropped bread, it will come true; however, if you've got a butter-side-down situation, it's bad luck. A butter-side-up scenario means a stranger will call.

FORK Dropping a fork means lady luck is on her way—or at the very least, a female guest. No downside here.

SPOON Dropped bowl side up, this is an invitation to good fortune. Bowl side down? Not so much.

KNIFE When a knife is accidentally dropped, if the point of the knife sticks in the floor, this is very good luck (not to mention dramatic). If it's leaning one way, odds are the good fortune will arrive from that direction. If the point doesn't stick in the floor, and the knife lands flat, it's bad luck; either a quarrel will follow or an unwelcome guest will call. If someone other than the person who dropped the knife picks it up, they will have good luck.

LUCKY LEFTOVERS

In England it's lucky to eat oysters, especially on August 5, St. James Day. Doing so ensures that the diner will never go hungry.

Tea for two doesn't mean that two people should pour from the same teapot. This is said to lead to arguments, and is almost as bad luck as pouring tea back into a teapot from a cup. To ensure good luck during teatime, always make sure the teakettle has a little water left in it.

If you're dining on a whole fish, eat it from head to tail for luck.

Bananas are extremely lucky fruit to Caribbean islanders. Make a wish while cutting a slice from the stalk end of the banana, and if you see a Y-shaped mark, your wish will be granted.

If you find one pea in a pod, it's considered good love luck. If you find nine peas in a pod, it's even better luck. Throw the whole thing over your shoulder, make a wish, and see if it comes true.

Dreaming of onions may be a sign that good luck is on its way.

If you're thinking of using that pair of chopsticks to do your best Lars Ulrich imitation, think again. It's bad luck to break chopsticks. It's also unlucky to stick a pair of chopsticks upright in a bowl of rice, since that resembles sticks of incense in a Buddhist funeral.

It's your lucky day if you break an egg that contains two yolks; wishes made on this egg are believed to come true. Eggs are generally lucky because they symbolize sacred reproductive powers, and two yolks mean that your good luck will be doubled.

DESTINATION LUCK

The world is filled with places that are known for being lucky. Travelers in search of good fortune can travel from Australia to Vegas visiting destinations where bells can be rung, statues rubbed, and bridges crossed—all to bring luck to the pilgrim. Following is a compendium of not only lucky destinations, but also lucky customs and beliefs from the four corners of the earth. We live in a lucky world, so it's time for you to grab your passport and go out and explore it! Or at least read about it.

NORTHERN
IRELAND

IRELAND

ENGLAND

GREAT BRITAIN AND IRELAND

FLIPPING THE DEVIL'S STONE
Shebbear, Devon

If you want to witness bad luck being overturned (literally), head to Shebbear in Devon on November 5 of any year. While everyone else in the country is celebrating Guy Fawkes Day, the citizens of this village have a much weightier matter at hand—the turning over of a six-foot-long stone said to have been "dropped by the devil" in the village square. No one is sure how the stone, which is not native to the region, actually came to be there, but it has been there since long before the village itself. To prevent bad luck befalling the village, the stone, which weighs more than a ton, has to be flipped over by the village bell ringers. This flipping ceremony is mentioned in the *Domesday Book* (c. 1086) and is said to be one of the oldest customs in all of Europe. At 8:00 p.m., the bells of the local church are rung, the stone is flipped, and everyone breathes a collective sigh of relief as good luck is assured. At least until the next year.

....

THE BLARNEY STONE
Blarney Castle, County Cork

Never at a loss for words herself, Queen Elizabeth I was the one responsible for the association between this castle, its famous stone, and the gift of off-the-cuff eloquence. Seemingly annoyed by all the smooth talk and excuses that the Lord of Blarney gave her when she tried to negotiate possession of his lands, the queen is said to have uttered something to the effect of, "It's all Blarney!" If you're willing to climb high into the battlements of this five-hundred-year-old castle, trust a stranger to hold you by the legs while you lie back over the parapet walk, and reach backward and give the fabled piece of limestone a kiss, you'll be rewarded with what some say is a particularly Irish kind of luck—the gift of gab.

NORTHERN IRELAND

THE WISHING CHAIR
Giants Causeway, County Antrim

Boasting rock formations made up of more than forty thousand hexagonal columns standing beneath the dramatic gray cliffs on the northern coast of Northern Ireland, this remarkable place looks like something straight out of a giant's playground. And, apparently, it is. Legend goes that a giant named Finn MacCool placed the rocks there as a way to form a walkway to Scotland, home of the woman he loved. At the tip of the middle causeway is a rocky seat known as the Wishing Chair, which was ostensibly made for Finn when he was a child. For visitors, it is believed that any wish made while seated in the chair will come true (although, given that, it's unclear why Finn didn't just wish his girlfriend would move to Ireland).

MONACO

STATUE OF KING LOUIS XV
Monte Carlo

MONTE CARLO

The Principality of Monaco has long reigned as one of the most glamorous places in the world to gamble. But before wagering your fortune at the Casino de Monte-Carlo, "where luck and chance go hand in hand," join gamblers in the know, and head first to the legendary Hôtel de Paris across the street, where you'll find in the lobby a large brass statue of King Louis XV atop his steed. Whether you're actually a high roller or just want to pretend you are, try rubbing the horse's knee or the king's nose. Either is said to ensure that the cards will be on your side.

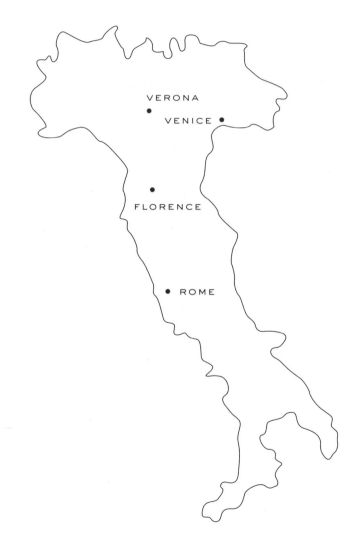

VERONA

VENICE

FLORENCE

ROME

ITALY

IL PORCELLINO
Florence

A seventeenth-century bronze statue made by Pietro Tacca resides in the Loggia del Mercato Nuovo. Although he is a *cinghiale* (wild boar), the locals refer to him as *il porcellino* (the piglet). Legend has it that if you rub his snout, it will bring you good luck. Some locals also suggest rolling a coin down the boar's nose or placing a coin in his mouth and letting it fall. If the coin falls directly into the grate of the fountain, it brings added luck.

....

THE BRIDGE OF SIGHS
Venice

Built in 1600 as a passageway between the Palazzo Ducale, the Doge's Palace, and the Palazzo delle Prigioni, where prisoners were held, this deceptively beautiful bridge supposedly got its name from the exhalations of prisoners as they were being led across the bridge to the executioner. Today, the only sighs you're likely to hear are from amorous couples, since the belief is that your luck in romance will last forever if you take a gondola ride at sunset with your lover and kiss while you pass directly underneath the bridge.

JULIET'S BALCONY
Verona

This serene courtyard in the heart of medieval Verona, tucked away at number 27 Via Cappello, is one of the most popular tourist attractions in the city. Here you can stare at the fabled balcony up which Romeo purportedly climbed to profess his love for Juliet. More importantly, you can join the millions of others who rub the right breast of the bronze statue of Juliet, sculpted by Nereo Constantini, believing it will bring eternal love and good luck in romance. Which is odd, really, if you think about how things turned out for her.

TREVI FOUNTAIN
Rome

If you're ever lucky enough to see this magnificent fountain, built by Niccolò Salvi in 1762, you'll also witness hundreds of tourists from all over the world jostling for position, standing with their backs to the fountain, and tossing coins over their shoulders into the splashing waters. It's really a testament to how beloved the city is to travelers, since the only luck you're said to receive from a slam dunk is the promise that you'll return to Rome again one day. Perhaps even luckier is the city of Rome, which collects an estimated three thousand euros every day in thrown money, which is used to subsidize a supermarket for those in need.

....

WHEN IN ROME

Don't run away if you're near a cat that is about to sneeze; it's good luck for anyone who hears it.

Keep your distance from houses with birds in them.

Don't compliment anyone on how beautiful his or her baby is; it evokes the *maloccio* (evil eye).

Ward off the evil eye with the *mano cornuto* (the sign of the horn), by extending your pinkie and index finger while keeping the thumb and other fingers folded down.

Stay away from nuns. If a nun can't be avoided, touch iron (knocking on wood Italian-style) immediately after seeing one to preserve good fortune. You can also do as the Italians do and mutter "Your nun!" to the next person you see, passing the nun (and therefore the bad luck) to someone else.

Avoid the number seventeen. Not only do the digits look like a man hanging from a gallows (the one being the man and the seven being the gallows); if you write the number out using Roman numerals, you get XVII. If you reorder these letters it spells out VIXI, which in Latin is the past tense for *live* and is the word that usually begins a tomb inscription.

Carry a bent nail in your pocket.

Wear a tiny horn-shaped charm (*cornetto*) around your neck to keep away bad fortune.

KIRUNA

LULEÅ

TÄRNABY

SKELLEFTEÅ

UMEÅ

SUNDSVALL

HUDIKSVALL

GÄVLE

UPPSALA

NORRTALJE

KARLSTAD

ÖREBRO

STOCKHOLM

GÖTEBORG

NORRKÖPING

BORÅS

JÖNKÖPING

HALMSTAD

HELSINGBORG

SÖLVESBORG

MALMÖ

SWEDEN

MANHOLE COVERS
Any street in Sweden

Don't be surprised if you see people weaving up and down the streets in a peculiar manner the next time you're in Stockholm. The streets are full of manholes, and plenty of Swedes believe that stepping on the manhole covers marked with a *k* is lucky, while stepping on the ones marked with an *a* is unlucky. Let us explain.

The *k* on manhole covers actually stands for *källvatten* (fresh water), but, to the believers of this lucky tradition, *k* stands for *kärlek* (love). When you step on a *k* manhole cover, you're supposed to think of the one you love, and it will bring good luck to the both of you. Jumping is also encouraged, as the more times you jump on the manhole, the better your luck in love will be. And it goes without saying that the luckiest thing you can ever do for your love life is to stand on a *k* and kiss.

The *a* stands for *avlopp* (sewage), and this leads to some pretty unlucky connotations for the Swedes: *a* for them can mean *avbruten* (broken love), *avundsjuka* (envy), or even act as a warning to "be aware" (*akta*). If you happen to step on an *a* manhole, the unlucky effects can be counteracted if someone pats you on the back three times. The catch is, they have to do this voluntarily, without being asked. Most prepubescent boys, however, step on the *a* and stay away from the *k* as much as possible—yuck, love!

CZECH REPUBLIC

THE CHARLES BRIDGE
Prague

Here's a bridge that was designed from the beginning to be lucky. To protect the new construction from powerful floodwaters that had destroyed the original bridge, the foundation stone was laid in 1357 on the 9th of July at 5:31 a.m., a date that forms a palindrome (135797531) and that was deemed by astrologers to be decidedly auspicious for King Charles IV. This lucky move seems to have paid off, as the picturesque bridge is still standing today, even under the stress of much more threatening forces—the thousands of tourists who storm it every day, making it Prague's leading attraction. Crowds make a beeline for the bridge's statue of St. John of Nepomuk to rub the brass relief plaque underneath for good luck.

....

POLAND

WAWEL CATHEDRAL
Krakow

The giant bell atop the Wawel Cathedral in Krakow (named the Zygmunt Bell, after the Polish king who donated it to the cathedral in 1520) is one of the largest bells in the world, and, on important holidays such as Christmas and Easter, its toll can be heard from as far as fifty miles away. But you're going to want to get much closer than that. It's worth the climb up the many stairs to the top of the bell tower to touch the 660-pound clapper, since doing so will bless you with good luck and may even grant you the wish that you whisper as you touch it.

SLOVENIA

CHURCH OF THE ASSUMPTION
Bled Island

On a tiny teardrop-shaped island in the middle of Lake Bled sits a baroque church straight out of a fairy tale. Ninety-nine steps stretch dramatically from the edge of the water to the front of the church, which sits at the top of a hill. The local wedding tradition calls for strapping husbands to carry their new brides up the steps to the church for good luck, during which time the bride must remain completely silent (undoubtedly the first and last time for *that* during the marriage). For those of you not getting married, there's something else you can do for good luck—take one of the *pletnas* (traditional wooden boats that resemble gondolas) out to the island, climb the stairs to the church, make a wish, and ring the "wish bell." Legend has it that those who ring the bell to honor the Blessed Virgin will see their wish come true.

FROM RUSSIA WITH LUCK

A woman with full water buckets coming
toward you is a sign of good luck, but if her
buckets are empty, it signals bad luck.

To ensure that luck is on your side, don't
make your bed, wear anything new, or cut your
fingernails on the day you have an exam.

Seeing a funeral procession brings good luck,
but you should never cross its path.

Found a bay leaf in your bowl of borscht?
Lucky you! You'll be getting good news in
the mail from someone soon.

For good luck when you travel, sit silently
for a moment beside your suitcases before leaving
the house. This is also a good opportunity to
think of anything you may have forgotten to pack.

Tripping on your left foot is a sign of good luck
(not that there's usually a choice in the matter).

Knock on wood three times for luck, but go
the extra mile and add three spits to your left to spit
on the devil, who is always seated to that side.

Don't put keys on the kitchen table; it's bad luck.

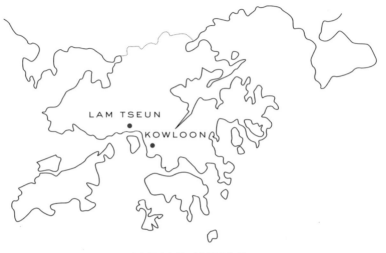

HONG KONG

LAM TSUEN WISHING TREES
Lam Tsuen

Regarded as gods, these two huge banyan trees are in the business of granting wishes. The larger tree is traditionally for wishing for luck in school, health, and career matters, while the smaller is for wishing for luck in love, marriage, and children. People in Hong Kong visit this lucky site near Tai Po year-round, but especially during Chinese New Year. To make a wish, you write your name and the wish on a colorful piece of paper, tie it to an orange, and toss it up into the tree. If it hangs on one of the branches, your wish will be granted. Some say you only get three tosses to make it stick, but if you have more oranges, the trees aren't going to stop you.

SIK SIK YUEN WONG TAI SIN TEMPLE
Kowloon

Anyone looking to change their luck (in health, business, or even gambling) is advised to come to this temple, which is named after a legendary shepherd boy who invented a magical cure when he was fifteen. The temple is famous for its fortune-tellers, whose favored technique is the reading of numbered sticks. The tellee shakes a bamboo container holding seventy-eight numbered sticks until one rises and eventually falls out. The teller then checks the number on that stick, cross-checks it with a chart of ancient texts, and reveals what it indicates for the future. Always a lucky hot spot, this temple gets especially jam-packed during Chinese New Year, when devotees from all over come to light joss sticks and pray for a successful year. Some even go at midnight on New Year's Eve, in order to be the first in line to receive the good luck of the brand-new year.

FOR THE CHINESE, LUCK IS IN THE NUMBERS

In the Chinese culture, certain numbers are believed to be lucky or unlucky based on what the word for the number sounds like. And certain numbers have such lucky associations that people will pay astronomical prices to obtain lucky-number combinations for their license plates and phone numbers, and even for the "right" address. Since there are hundreds of different dialects in the Chinese language, the luck factor varies according to where you are, but the general rules governing the beliefs are the same. The luckiest numbers include:

Pronounced "san," it sounds like the word for *life*, so it's always a lucky number.

Pronounced "liu," it sounds like the word for *smooth* and is considered lucky since it portends "everything going smoothly" in life as well as in business. You'll see "lucky" 666 in many shop windows across China, which may come as a shock to believers in the Beast and those with hexakosioihexekontahexaphobia.

Pronounced "ba," this is the luckiest number of all, since in both Mandarin and Cantonese it sounds similar to the word for *wealth* or *fortune*. This number is used to boost prosperity throughout China; the Bank of China always assigns its trading rooms to the eighth floor of its buildings, and China's tallest skyscraper, the Jin Mao Tower, is eighty-eight floors high. The Cantonese-speaking Hong Kongers especially value the number eight, and eighty-eight-dollar fixed-price menus are found in restaurants all over the island.

Pronounced "jeou," it sounds like the word for *long-lasting* and is a lucky number to have because it represents longevity in every aspect of life.

Four is a dreaded number all over Asia since it sounds like the word for *death* in many Asian languages. Companies that produce electronic gadgets such as cell phones often skip over the number when naming their product lines, and many buildings don't have a fourth floor. Even unluckier to the Cantonese is the number fourteen, since the pronunciation "sap sei" is dangerously close to "sat sei," which means "certainly going to die."

TORI NO ICHI FAIR

Otori shrines throughout Japan

The annual Tori no Ichi Fair has taken place on the "Rooster Days" of November since the 1700s (check local listings since the dates change every year). The patron saint of good fortune and successful business is enshrined at these Otori shrines, and the biggest of the fairs takes place at the Otori Shrine in Asakusa, Tokyo. Although many things about the fair are fun, most people go with the intention of buying a *kumade* (bamboo rake), which will rake in good luck for rakers and their businesses during the upcoming year. Certain shrewd regulars recommend attending the fair every year and, like some car owners, purchasing an upgraded model annually.

MOUNT FUJI
Shizuoka

To the Japanese, perhaps the luckiest sight in the world is the view of the sunrise from the summit of Mount Fuji. The mountain, Japan's highest at 12,388 feet, looms large in the Japanese psyche—it is the country's national symbol and a revered, sacred mountain that many dream of climbing. They also hope to dream of the mountain on the first day of the brand-new year, since doing so means that they will have luck all year long. You can join the huge numbers of trekkers who make the climb every summer, but don't be fooled by fellow climbers—for example, the seventy-eight-year-old grandmother of six—who would make you believe that climbing Fuji-san is a breeze. It's a strenuous, challenging climb and, as the saying goes, "A wise man climbs Fuji once, but only a fool would climb it twice."

SENSOJI TEMPLE
Asakusa, Tokyo

Hop on the subway to Tokyo's bustling district of Asakusa and visit the Sensoji Temple, which is protected by Fujin, the god of wind, and Raijin, the god of thunder. Before entering the temple, stop by the incense burner, the smoke of which will protect you from illness and give you good luck. Direct the smoke at the part of yourself where you need the most help—your head if you're a student, your face if you're an aging fashion model, and so on. Then a quick washing with holy water and you're ready to tour the temple. For a small fee you can have your fortune told by shaking a numbered stick from a cylinder. Each numbered stick corresponds to one of many numbered drawers built into a booth between the temple gates and the temple. If the fortune you pull from the drawer is a good one, hang onto it. If it's bad, tie it to the nearby metal rack to instantly counteract the negative prediction.

DAIROKUTEN-NO-HADAKA MATSURI
(aka The Naked Mudslinging Festival)
Musubi-jinja Shrine in Yotsukaido, Chiba

Naked mudslinging, anyone? Well, nearly naked mudslinging. This small, chilly festival, meant to bring good luck to the participants, the spectators, the community, and most of all the upcoming harvest, takes place each February 25. Local men clad in loincloths gather in a shallow, cold pond to wrestle, sling some mud, and put on an entertaining show for the gathered crowd. They'll also paint a little mud on your baby's face for good luck if you like and, as they run back and forth in the cold to and from the warming fires, they'll likely spread a little mud on your face for good luck, too. People proudly wear the muddy fingerprints on their cheeks for the day, perhaps just feeling lucky that it isn't them running around in the freezing cold wearing only a loincloth.

WHEN IN JAPAN

Dreaming of Mount Fuji, hawks, or eggplants
on the first night of the brand-new year means
you will have good luck all year long.

When giving gifts in multiples (such as candies,
dishes, etc.), do so in odd quantities, and *never* in fours.

Don't cut your nails at night, for it's believed if you
do that your parents will die before you see them again.
Although it seems unlikely, this is the most commonly
believed superstition in the country.

If someone is talking in their sleep, just let them be.
Talking back to them only invites bad luck.

It's bad luck if you break a comb or the strap of your sandals.

If you wear any new shoes at night, bad luck will come.

Avoid stepping on the cloth border of tatami floor mats.
Even with your shoes off, it's bad luck.

Pay attention to the first person you meet each
morning. If it's a woman, you'll have good luck, but if
it's a Buddhist priest, you're in for a bad day.

Seeing a spider in the morning is a sign of
good luck—just be careful not to step on it. Seeing
one at night is bad luck, so squish away.

Men should work extra hard to avoid bad luck at ages
twenty-five and forty-two, while women should watch out at
nineteen and thirty-three. These ages are called *yakudoshi*.
The word *yaku* means "calamity," and without a lot of care you
could be heading for disaster. Wearing red is supposed to help.

Serve sea bream on important occasions
for good luck since it is known in Japanese as *tai*,
which is part of the word *medetai* (good luck).

Hide your thumb in your fist when a hearse passes by.
This brings good luck to your parents, because your thumb
in Japanese is literally the "parent finger," and if
you hide it from the hearse, your parents will live longer.

The snake is a symbol of money and wealth, so a
snakeskin wallet is a great idea for attracting prosperity.

Pine, bamboo, and plums are considered a lucky combination,
and the same goes for cranes and turtles. When giving
a wedding present, tie the shape of a crane or turtle to the
ribbon. They bring good luck and long life to a marriage.

THAILAND

ERAWAN SHRINE
Bangkok

This small open-air shrine is one of the busiest, thanks to the miracles attributed to the site. People come here day and night to ask for good luck in exams, good luck in business, and good luck in just about everything else. Traditional Thai dancers are almost always on hand, and you can pay them to perform in front of the shrine to help your request stand out in the crowd. The shrine is dedicated to a Brahma god named Than Tao Mahaprom, but the name comes from Erawan, the three-headed elephant he rides on. When wishes are granted, people return with offerings of wooden elephants big and small.

WAT PO—TEMPLE OF THE RECLINING BUDDHA
Bangkok

One of Bangkok's most spectacular attractions is this three-hundred-year-old temple, the oldest and largest in the city. Inside is an immense golden statue of a reclining Buddha, installed more than two hundred years ago, measuring forty-nine feet high and more than one hundred and fifty feet long. Here you can follow the Thai lucky custom of buying a bag of coins and placing a coin into each of the 112 pots that line the length of the statue. If you feel like gold-plating your luck, you can buy a small piece of gold leaf to add to the Buddha's surface.

BURMA

VIETNAM

THAILAND

LINGAM SHRINE
Bangkok

Its location, tucked away at the back of the Nai Lert Park Swissotel, doesn't quite prepare you for what you'll come upon when you find this shrine: penises. Thousands of penises. Sculpted in every size, color, and shape imaginable, and some, like the ones with legs and tails, previously unimagined. Also known as Tuptim Shrine, it was originally built for a spirit who was believed to reside in a large banyan tree on the site. At some point devotees began placing phallic-shaped offerings all around, and the idea caught on. Today, the place is bursting with them, and it's no surprise that visiting the shrine is said to provide women with good luck in fertility.

THAI LUCKY COLORS

Many Thais believe that a color is assigned to every day of the week and wearing *that* color on *that* day will bring good luck. Your luckiest color is the one that corresponds with the day you were born, and it's the custom of many Thai (principally men) to pay homage to King Bhumibol Adulyadej by wearing a yellow shirt on Mondays, in honor of the day the king was born. Next time you're in Bangkok, you might find that your day goes better if you wear the following colors.

Monday: yellow or cream, Tuesday: pink, Wednesday: green,
Wednesday night: light green, Thursday: orange or brown,
Friday: blue, Saturday: purple or black, and Sunday: red

VIETNAM

PERFUME PAGODA
Huong Son

A couple of hours southwest of Hanoi, in the Huong Son mountain range and accessible only by boat, the Perfume Pagoda is one of Vietnam's most sacred sites. After a scenic ride along a stream that weaves through some of Vietnam's most unspoiled territory, visitors are led up an ancient flight of steps to a large limestone cave, where the shrine is situated. The cave itself is said to be lucky, and different kinds of luck—from luck in the form of prosperity to luck for your animals—are attributed to each stalactite and stalagmite. One stalactite in particular attracts thousands of couples to the cave every year, since the dripping water is supposed to bring good luck to those trying to conceive. If having a child is not on your agenda, you might want to wear protective rain gear (or at least a condom).

TEMPLE OF LITERATURE
Hanoi

Every July, Hanoi's 938-year-old Temple of Literature is jammed with thousands of stressed-out students hoping to pass their university entrance exams. The Temple is Vietnam's oldest university, and students come here to burn incense and touch the heads of the eighty-two sacred stone turtles that represent past university laureates, hoping some of their good luck will rub off. Many students even eat a "lucky breakfast" of green beans on the morning of the exam, since the Vietnamese word for *bean* is also the same word for *pass*. With 1.8 million candidates taking the test every year and only three hundred thousand places available in Vietnam's universities, hopefuls need every bit of luck they can get.

....

BURMA (MYANMAR)

MOUNT POPA
Popa

Mount Popa is the revered mystical mountain of Burma, and it is also home to the *nats*. Not to be confused with those tiny, annoying insects, *nats* are the spirits of folk heroes and dead nobles. Since pre-Buddhist times, the Burmese have made the pilgrimage up the precipitous steps of this extinct volcano to make offerings to them at the main shrine, named after Min Mahagiri, or "Lord of the Great Mountain." The views from the peak are spectacular, and the ancient temple is an architectural marvel that boasts figurines representing the thirty-seven *nats*. But here are some things you should *nat* do, sorry, *not* do if you make the trek up: don't curse; don't say anything negative about other people; don't wear black or red; and most importantly, don't carry any meat (especially pork). Any misstep will incur the wrath of the *nats* and unleash a flood of bad luck on you, which is the last thing you need after schlepping up a mountain.

BHUTAN

PARO FESTIVAL
Paro

Imagine being in the immense courtyard of a fortified monastery, watching monks in fearsome masks and brilliantly colored costumes executing dance moves with acrobatic precision as they reenact the legends and history of Buddhism. These dances, known as *cham*, aren't staged by some savvy tourist board for the benefit of tourists. They are part of an ancient blessing ritual that has remained unchanged for centuries, and if you happen to witness one during a *tshechu*, or "traditional festival," the luck's on you—the Bhutanese believe that simply witnessing this spectacle will bestow good luck and protect against misfortune. The Paro Festival, which takes place every spring, is the most popular one, and it's a great time to visit, since all the mountain flowers will be in full bloom.

INDIA

KARNI MATA TEMPLE
Deshnok

The Karni Mata Temple is infested with rats, thousands of rats. And that's the whole point. Here, the rodents, known as *kaba*, are believed to house the souls of the departed followers of Shri Karni Mata, who herself was the incarnation of the Hindu goddess Durga. And so the rats are worshipped as lucky deities and have free run of the temple. Big black and brown rats scamper unafraid everywhere—darting along the floors, crawling over visitors, lapping up milk from large shallow bowls, and nibbling at the food offerings put out for them. Most special of all is the single white rat that lives in the temple. To catch a glimpse of this elusive rat is good luck, and if it looks back at you, that's even luckier. It hardly needs saying that if you're crazy enough to pet the sacred white rat, you'll be the luckiest of all.

TASHIDING MONASTERY
Sikkim

The breathtaking Indian state of Sikkim is a remote Himalayan Shangri-La neighboring Tibet and Nepal. There you can visit the illustrious Tashiding Monastery, which houses one of the most holy *chortens* in the Buddhist world. *Chortens* are traditional Buddhist structures in South Asia that are akin to pagodas. This one is known as Thong-Wa-rang-Dol, which literally means "saviors by mere sight." All you have to do is to look at the *chorten* and the mere sight of it will cleanse your soul, wash it free of all sins, and infuse you with good luck. (Unfortunately, it's an awfully long way to go after a rough Saturday night and too many appletinis.) The monastery also holds an annual festival known as the Bumchu Ceremony, which brings in devotees from far and wide wishing to benefit from the lucky blessings of the holy water from the temple.

NEPAL

MUKTINATH TEMPLE
District of Mustang

At an altitude of almost 12,500 feet above sea level sits the temple of Muktinath, or "God of Nirvana." It's a sacred pilgrimage site to both Hindus and Buddhists, and a prime example of how two religions can share the same holy shrine with mutual respect and harmony. It is said that all miseries and sorrows are relieved once you have visited the temple, which is dedicated to the Lord Vishnu. The secret to this may lie in the temple's semicircular courtyard, where 108 brass waterspouts shaped like bulls' heads stream out a continuous flow of holy water. For the devotees who make the long trek to Muktinath, the fresh, invigorating (and freezing) Himalayan waters are not only a cleansing and purifying reward, they are said to wash away all negative karma. The number 108 is a very auspicious one in both Hindu and Buddhist mythology, so for good luck, make sure to bathe under each of the 108 spigots. If you can't handle a full-on bath in subzero water, try a quick splash underneath each.

TO CUBA

BRAZIL

BOLIVIA

BOLIVIA

WITCHES' MARKET
La Paz

If you're running low on boa constrictor heads (and who isn't?), head straight to the Mercado de las Brujas, or "Witches' Market," for a refill. Snaking along the Calle Linares in the old quarter of La Paz, this teeming cobblestone street is where folk doctors, medicine women, astrologers, and tourists alike flock when they need to find the latest assortment of charms, talismans, spells, and cures. You can get your fortune read with coco leaves or poke your way around the crowded stalls, where friendly witches in colorful dresses and signature bowler hats will happily show you their wares. Llama fetuses are the perennial hot seller; it's said that 99 percent of all Bolivians place one in the foundations of their houses for good luck, and they are also burnt as lucky offerings for new business ventures. This may not be Diagon Alley, but it's probably the closest thing you'll find to it in this world.

BRAZIL

LUCKY NEW YEAR'S EVE

Brazil is the uncontested ruler of New Year's celebrations around the world and, from the tiniest village to the largest city, Brazilians turn the volume up to eleven when it comes to marking New Year's. One need only witness the scene on Copacabana Beach in Rio de Janeiro every December 31, when a million revelers dressed in white take to the waves, in order to be convinced. Here's a guide to the simpatías, *which are the lucky dos and don'ts, if you plan to ring in New Year's Brazilian style.*

....

DEFINITELY WORTH TRYING

Eat lentils, pork, dates, and hard-shelled nuts.

....

Jump three times while holding a glass of champagne and then toss the champagne behind you. Whoever gets splashed is said to be in luck.

....

Fill your house with yellow flowers for prosperity.

Suck on seven pomegranate seeds and save them in your wallet for a full year to ensure good fortune.

....

Wear white and only white. This color originates from the Candomblé rituals of the Afro-Brazilians, but everyone has adopted this custom, regardless of their beliefs.

Have your right foot raised when the clock strikes midnight, so that your first step into the brand-new year is the right one.

Be sure you sleep in new bed sheets after your night of partying, for good luck in your relationship.

Pucker up and kiss someone at the stroke of midnight. If you're single, just grab the nearest person and kiss away—most Brazilians won't mind.

Head down to the beach and jump over seven small waves in a row.

DON'T EVER

Serve chicken for New Year's; it won't bring you abundance in the coming year.

Start the year on the wrong foot by putting down your left foot first.

Wear old clothes, as this brings bad luck.

Wear black underwear or underwear that you've bought for yourself.

Go penniless. You should have a little bit of lucky money in your pocket or tucked in your shoe.

Start the year with a dirty or messy house.

PANTY CODE (FOR LADIES ONLY)

Brazilian women believe that the color of the underwear they wear on New Year's Eve can help them fulfill specific wishes for the year ahead. So be sure to pick panties that match what you desire most. Luckily none of this requires that you get a Brazilian bikini wax.

RED	⟶	PASSION
PINK	⟶	LOVE
YELLOW	⟶	PROSPERITY
GREEN	⟶	LUCK
BLUE	⟶	TRANQUILITY
VIOLET	⟶	SPIRITUALITY

NB: This code only applies to women, since most Brazilian men are too macho to care about the color of their underwear.

CUBAN LUCK

Throw a bucket of ice with water out the front door at
midnight on New Year's Eve for good luck.

Keep San Lazaro (the patron saint of lepers) happy by
lighting up a cigar and blowing the smoke in the
face of your San Lazaro statue—he enjoys a good smoke.

During the new moon, take a coin and make
the sign of the cross with it while looking at the moon.
This ensures you good-luck money.

If you fear that someone might do you harm, write
that person's name on a piece of paper, fold it up,
and put it in the freezer to freeze away any bad luck.

Throw ice on the floor while cleaning it. It's supposed to
cool the house down and cleanse it with good luck.

During a bad storm, pray to Santa Barbara, who also doubles
as Chango (not Charo, that crazy lady who was always on
The Love Boat), the Santería god of thunder, for lucky protection.

Put pennies in the soil of fern plants and place them
all around your house to attract prosperity luck.

Say a lucky Cuban toast: *Salud, Amor y Pesetas*!
(Health, love, and money!)

LUCKY LATIN SUITCASE

*Throughout Latin America, people wishing to travel take part in
a custom during New Year's to assure that they will be lucky enough
to make the trip of their dreams or travel as much as they want in the
coming year. It's unclear where this tradition first originated, but from
Cuba to Colombia, would-be jet-setters practice the lucky ritual.
So whether you're filled with wanderlust or just trying to get away from
it all, follow these simple and fun instructions for lucky travels.*

....

 Think of the country (or countries) that you'd like to visit in the coming year.

 Before New Year's Eve, pack a suitcase with all the things you'll need on your trip there. If you're heading for the Swiss Alps, for example, be sure to pack your warm scarf, ski goggles, and packets of hot chocolate.

 At the stroke of midnight on New Year's Eve, grab the packed suitcase and run around your block with it.

 If you're really desperate to get away, try circling the block three times like some people do to lock in the luck.

5   *¡Buen viaje!*

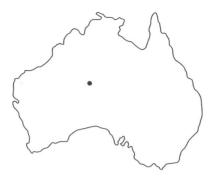

AUSTRALIA

ULURU—KATA TJUTA NATIONAL PARK
Yulara Northern Territory

Uluru, also known as Ayers Rock, is the most sacred place of the Aboriginal Australians and, fittingly, is situated at the very center of Australia. As the world's largest monolith, Uluru has attracted millions of visitors, who have been impressed by both its physical and spiritual qualities. Visiting Uluru, and especially dreaming about it, is said to bring good luck. But many who have wanted to take home part of their experience haven't been so lucky. Over the years, thousands of rocks have been returned to the national park's staff from all over the world. The senders have claimed that they were plagued by bad luck in the form of everything from poor health to failed marriages since removing the souvenir rocks. Rocks are sometimes returned with letters of apology, and, to discourage first-time visitors from making the same mistake, park managers have taken to displaying selected tales of woe along with the stolen rocks, now dubbed "conscience rocks." So visit it, enjoy it, but definitely leave for home without it.

NEW YORK

PENNSYLVANIA

NEVADA

LOUISIANA

FLORIDA

MASSACHUSETTS

HAWAII

NB: States in red are not necessarily Republican.

UNITED STATES OF AMERICA

THE TREE OF LOVE
St. Augustine, Florida

Tucked away on a leafy corner of St. Augustine, at number 6 Cordova Street, is the Tree of Love, two trees that seem to be entwined in a torrid testament of botanic codependency. Actually, it's a palm tree that's been growing through the middle of an oak tree for more than 125 years, and legend has it that if you kiss your loved one under the tree, you'll have guaranteed good luck for your relationship for the rest of eternity. For the six-dollar entry fee, it's worth a try.

BENJAMIN FRANKLIN'S GRAVE
Philadelphia, Pennsylvania

Many visitors to Ben Franklin's burial place follow the local tradition of tossing a penny on his grave for good luck. Even though his grave is one of the simpler ones at Christ Church Burial Ground, you'll find it easily—just look for the one littered with coins. Franklin is famously misquoted as having said, "A penny saved is a penny earned," while what he actually said was "A penny saved is two pence dear." Either way, it basically means the same thing, and it makes you wonder what he would have thought about all of this coin-throwing business.

Las Vegas, Nevada

*In this city where your fortunes can change at the drop of a chip,
there's no shortage of places you can go to double down your luck.*

....

BUDDHA STATUE
California Hotel and Casino

This happy Buddha's tummy glistens from all the good-luck patting
it has received over the years. The statue is especially popular with
Asian tourists, who drape him with leis or leave coin offerings in
hopes that their winnings will grow bigger than his belly.

....

HEADLESS LENIN STATUE
Mandalay Bay

This decapitated statue owes its fate to the many military personnel
who complained about its presence outside of the Red Square restaurant at Mandalay Bay. These days, you can find Lenin's head frozen
inside a block of ice in the walk-in freezer next to the bar, and giving
his headless body a slap is supposed to make you the supreme dictator
of any gaming table.

"CRAZY GIRLS" STATUE
Riviera Hotel

Weighing in at 1,540 pounds, Michael Conine's bronze statue of seven Vegas showgirls lined up in a row, with their derrières exposed, is cheekily named *No Ifs, Ands, Or.* . . . Give each of their shiny butts a rub for luck. It's the one grope in Vegas that won't cost you a dime.

....

BRAHMA SHRINE
Caesars Palace

If you're germophobic, here's a lucky spot you don't have to rub. This eight-thousand-pound replica of Thailand's most popular Buddhist shrine was crafted in Thailand and shipped to the resort for assembly. It's the only one of its kind in the Western Hemisphere, and it's believed that making a wish in front of the statue will bring prosperity.

....

ELVIS PRESLEY STATUE
Las Vegas Hilton

No visit to Vegas is complete without paying homage to the King. This life-size bronze by Carl Romanelli commands the entrance of the hotel, where Elvis performed 837 consecutive sold-out shows. Rubbing anywhere along his bell-bottomed legs should get you all shook up and ready to roll the dice!

THE BULL OF WALL STREET
New York, New York

The *Charging Bull* is a seven-thousand-pound bronze sculpture of (you guessed it) a charging bull by artist Arturo Di Modica. Wall Street traders make a point of walking past the bull every morning and rubbing a certain part of its anatomy (hint: not its nose) for luck before they take to the trading floor. If you handle your own stocks, consider making a pilgrimage to Manhattan's Financial District to rub the animal yourself—it might just give you the luck you need to beat the street.

APOLLO THEATER'S TREE OF HOPE
New York, New York

The Apollo Theater in Harlem has launched the careers of many music stars, and this might have something to do with the Tree of Hope. This elm tree originally stood outside the Harlem Lafayette Theater on Seventh Avenue. Performers believed standing under the tree would bring them luck. When the avenue was widened, the tree was chopped down, cut up, and pieces were sold off as lucky souvenirs. One buyer was Ralph Cooper Sr., originator of Amateur Night at the Apollo, who bought a log, shellacked it, and placed it stage right at the theater. If you happen to be lucky enough to appear at the Apollo, be sure to rub the log for good luck on your way to center stage.

STATUE OF JOHN HARVARD
Cambridge, Massachusetts

Outside University Hall sits a bronze statue of John Harvard. The statue is popularly known by Harvard tour guides as the "Statue of Three Lies," since the plaque on the statue proclaiming him as the founder in 1638 is laden with three inaccuracies: Harvard wasn't actually the founder of America's oldest institute of higher learning—the college was started by the government and named for Harvard after he bequeathed a library to it. The college was founded in 1636, not 1638. And, perhaps most embarrassing, the man in the statue isn't even John Harvard. Harvard died without a good likeness, so the sculptor Daniel Chester French had a model sit in for him, long after his death, in 1884. Despite, or perhaps even because of, these blunders, many students believe that rubbing the foot of the statue will bring good luck during their exams. The statue is even more popular with tourists, who rub and kiss its foot, possibly hoping that the luck of those fortunate enough to get into Harvard will rub off on them. Rub it, pat it, and have your picture taken with it by all means, but we don't recommend kissing it, since it's said that Harvard Yard's most beloved statue by day becomes its most popular urinal after dark.

MARIE LAVEAU'S GRAVE
New Orleans, Louisiana

At Saint Louis Cemetery Number One, Crypt Number Three stands a curious tomb. Numerous X-shaped markings are scratched onto the walls, and littered all around are candles, Mardi Gras beads, food, and other paraphernalia. This is the grave of Marie Laveau or, at least, it's reputed to be. Much of Laveau's legend is obscured by more than a century of myth, but by the time she died in 1881 she had long reigned as New Orleans's most famous and feared voodoo priestess. Mixing voodoo spells with Roman Catholic beliefs, Laveau pioneered a new hybrid form of voodoo that made the practice more palatable to white Creole Catholics. Today, thousands flock to her grave every year to make wishes and offerings and to ask for good luck. In the past, people would take a piece of the crumbling red brick found in the cemetery and scratch Laveau's grave with three cross marks (XXX) for luck. Since the tomb has become ever more fragile because of this practice, we recommend following another tradition—just knock three times on the tomb to receive good luck from this legendary queen of voodoo.

ALOHA LUCK

*Travelers to Hawaii tend to be so swept up in the fun,
sand, surf, and beauty of it all that they forget that the Islands
are home to their own set of lucky rules. Here are some
essential tips to keep the lucky island gods on your side.*

....

Don't remove any lava rocks from the Islands. It's said to anger Pele,
the Hawaiian volcano goddess, and will bring very bad luck.

Grow a ti plant at home; it's the good-luck plant of
Hawaii and will attract good fortune into your home.

Don't take pork over the Pali Highway in Oahu or risk
bad luck (or, at the very least, car trouble). According to legend,
Pele had a tormented relationship with her lover, the demigod
Kamapua'a, who was half man and half hog, so the two
agreed to stay on separate parts of the island. If you take pork
over the Pali, you are said to be taking a piece of Kamapua'a to
Pele's side of the island—something she will never let happen.

It's unlucky to bring bananas onto a boat.

To keep good luck on your side, don't wear a lei if you're pregnant.

Rainbows bring good luck. To this day, the University
of Hawaii football team (formerly the Rainbow Warriors)
looks for a rainbow over the Manoa Valley before a game,
as the appearance of one means an assured victory.

WISH ME LUCK

*On your travels abroad, you never know when it might come in
handy to wish locals "good luck" in their native tongue.**

Afrikaans	*Veels geluck; Sterkte*
Arabic	*Hathan mwafakan*
Catalan	*Bona sort*
Chinese	*Zhu ni hao yun*
Danish	*Held og lykke*
Dutch	*Veel succes gewenst*
Finnish	*Onnea*
French	*Bonne chance*
German	*Viel glück*
Greek	*Kali tihi*
Hawaiian	*Maika'i Pomaika'i*
Hebrew	*Mazl tov; B'hatzlacha*
Hindi	*Shubh kamnaye*
Hungarian	*Sok szerencsét kivánok*
Icelandic	*Gangi pér vel*
Indonesian	*Semoga beruntung*
Italian	*Buona fortuna; In bocca al lupo*

**Many believe that saying "good luck" is actually bad luck since it's tempting fate. But
sometimes it's the only thing that seems appropriate. Just be sure after you say it that you
knock on wood to offset any bad luck you may incur by bringing it up in the first place.*

Irish	*Go n-éirí an t-ádh leat*
Japanese	*Gambatte*
Korean	*Heng unid bimnida*
Lithuanian	*Laimingai*
Malaysian	*Semoga berjaya*
Norwegian	*Lykke til*
Persian	*Movaffag bashid*
Polish	*Powodzenia*
Portuguese	*Boa sorte*
Russian	*Zhela(iu)(em) udachi*
Serbo-Croatian	*Svetno*
Spanish	*Buena suerte*
Swedish	*Lycka till*
Tagalog	*Mabuting kapalaran*
Thai	*Kor hai chok dee*
Turkish	*Iyi talih*
Vietnamese	*Chue may man*
Yiddish	*Zol zayn mit mazl*
Zulu	*Ngikufisela izilokotho ezinhle*

EVERYDAY LUCK

SUN	MON	TUE	WED	THU	FRI	SAT
	1	2	3	4	5	6
7						13
14						20
21						27
28	29	30	31			

This is a practical guide to bringing good luck into your life in every situation and on every occasion. Whether you're planning a special event, starting a new venture, or simply looking for a way to improve your golf game, these pages will provide you with tips you can use to enhance your luck. And don't forget, there are no hard-and-fast rules. A lucky law that applies to your car will probably work just as well for your Vespa, and a tip for winning at poker might be just the thing for the office pool.

LIFE'S BIG MOMENTS

THE RULES OF ENGAGEMENT

So, you think you want to get married . . .

....

DEFINITELY WORTH TRYING

Buy an engagement ring that includes the bride's birthstone.

Want to propose to your man? February 29 is the date set
for just that purpose. It only comes once every four years,
so be sure to grab the opportunity when it's there.

Pick the day of the week for your proposal wisely—
it will likely affect the kind of life you'll have together.
Monday = lively; Tuesday = peaceful; Wednesday = quarrel free;
Thursday = successful; Friday = hardworking; Saturday = pleasurable;
but you'll want to stay away from Sunday altogether.

Although it's hard to imagine accepting a proposal from your
boyfriend's frat buddy, it's always been considered lucky to
have a proposal delivered by a person other than the groom.

Seal the engagement by drinking a toast together
from the same glass, pinkies locked.

Break a plate or glass to symbolize the break
from your days as a singleton.

DON'T EVER

Propose on a moving vehicle, a boat, a train, or a Sunday.

Buy an engagement ring with an opal or pearl in it.
Opals are changeable and signal instability, and pearls
mean tears are to follow.

Buy a ring without figuring out her size in advance.
Having to adjust a ring is unlucky.

Let anyone other than the bride try on the engagement ring.
Bride-to-be, you can let your envious friends give it a whirl;
just don't let them push it past their first knuckle.

Lose or break the engagement ring—it foretells an unhappy ending.

Let someone photograph you between the first day
of your engagement and the wedding day.

Agree to stand as godparents while engaged, particularly at a
baptism. An old saying goes, "First at the font, never at the altar."

Change your wedding date once it's been decided.

CALLING IT QUITS

If you want to call it off, present your spouse-not-to-be with a knife
(handle first, and caaaarefully) to cut the ties of the relationship.

WEDDING

Finding the love of your life is certainly lucky, and here are a few ways to make sure the marriage begins auspiciously.

....

DEFINITELY WORTH TRYING

Plan your wedding to take place before sundown.

....

Brides, be sure to feed the cat, if you have one, before you leave your house on your wedding day; it's good luck.

....

Ribbons with knots are lucky additions to bridal bouquets, as they catch and hold love.

....

Make sure that the bride is wearing something old, something new, something borrowed, and something blue. And often added to the rhyme is "a penny in her shoe," which is extra lucky when given to the bride by the groom.

A pin from the wedding dress is good luck to whoever obtains it; just be sure the bride doesn't still need it!

....

Putting orange blossoms in the bride's hair or on her veil is considered lucky, since the orange tree is known to bear fruit and blossoms at the same time.

....

It's best luck for the marriage if the wedding party approaches the ceremony venue from a clockwise direction.

....

Throwing rice or confetti at the wedded couple is considered good luck, notably in matters related to fertility.

Untie the groom's shoelaces before he walks down the aisle to be sure that night's events are without obstacles. Just be sure you tell him first.

....

It's also lucky to throw an old shoe after (not at) the wedded couple, or to tie shoes (or tin cans) to the fender of the car they are departing in.

....

Hire a chimney sweep to kiss the bride or walk with the wedding couple.

....

The bridal bouquet and garter make lucky catches for bridesmaids and groomsmen looking to get hitched. Touching the bride or groom is also thought to bring luck to the love seeker.

The bride and groom should cut the cake together, with the groom's hand over hers. It will bring her happiness and fortune that he will then share in.

....

Have a wedding cake! It's a symbol of fortune and is lucky for everyone who has a slice.

....

Every new bride should be carried over the threshold on the first night of the honeymoon and then again when the couple return home.

....

Save either the top layer of your wedding cake or a generous slice in your freezer, and share it with your spouse on your first-year wedding anniversary for good luck.

DON'T EVER

Let the bride or groom leave their respective homes via the back door on the way to the wedding.

Allow the bridal party to run into a funeral on the way to the ceremony.

Let the bride look at herself in her entire wedding outfit before the wedding. She should always leave off a glove or shoe. And she should never try on the veil and the wedding dress at the same time.

Let the groom see the bride in her gown before the ceremony.

Drop the ring! And at all costs, not during the ceremony, which is considered very unlucky.

Refuse to partake of the cake (it's bad luck for the wedding couple and the refusenik).

Give the couple knives as a gift.

Agree to be a bridesmaid more than twice ("Three times a bridesmaid, never a bride"). If it can't be avoided it, shoot for seven times, at which point the bad luck turns to good.

HONEYMOON

*It's no coincidence that the most significant lucky tradition
having to do with the honeymoon has to do with, well, honey.
But there are also a few other lucky tips to follow.*

DEFINITELY WORTH TRYING

Although it was once traditional for the happy couple to drink mead (a fermented drink made with honey) for a full cycle of the moon after the wedding, adding honey to any beverage you drink (like tea or lemonade) for the first thirty days of your marriage will bring luck.

Grooms, close and lock the door on the wedding night to avoid arguments.

Go to Niagara Falls and toss a coin into Bridal Veil Falls (on the U.S. side) or Horseshoe Falls (on the Canadian side) for luck.

OK, want to go somewhere slightly more exotic than upstate New York? Casting a coin into a fountain, well, or any other body of water while on your honeymoon will ensure a happy marriage.

DON'T EVER

Tell anyone where you're going on your honeymoon.

Fall asleep first on your wedding night. Whoever does will be the first to die. But really, who's even thinking about sleep?

CONCEPTION, BIRTH, AND BABIES

Nothing can match the joy of bringing a new life, filled with luck,
into the world (except maybe a nice bag of Cheetos).

DEFINITELY WORTH TRYING

Frogs are lucky symbols of fertility and abundance, due to the large quantity of eggs they lay at a time. So purchase a frog charm and keep it by your bedside when trying to conceive.

The expectant mother should throw salt three times behind her shortly before her due date in order to ease her labor.

A baby born via breech delivery is said to be unusually lucky.

Both a first-born child and a baby born with a caul (which sounds grosser than it actually is) are thought to be lucky.

Unlock doors and windows, and undo any knots in shoelaces or drapery to ease delivery.

Although nothing beats a good epidural, keep a knife under the maternity bed to help ease the pain of childbirth.

"Give a dog a bad name and you might as well hang him" goes an old saying, so be careful when picking your baby's name. A bad name is sure to bring bad luck. We don't really know what constitutes a bad name, but we think if your last name is Head, naming your son Richard might be an example.

Although it will make many a new parent reach for the bottle of antibacterial soap, spitting on a baby will bring him good luck.

....

Make sure you bring the baby up in the world before bringing her down. If you happen to have given birth on the top floor, mounting a stepladder or chair (again, caaaarefully) with the baby in your arms before heading downstairs will do the trick.

....

A baby's first sneeze is considered lucky; it blows out any evil.

....

Have a good-tempered person be the first to kiss your newborn so your baby is lucky enough to grow up to be a happy person.

....

Kissing a newborn is lucky for anyone who does so.

Wrapping your new baby in something old will swaddle him with good luck.

....

Dress your baby starting with her feet rather than first pulling something over her head.

....

If you've invited guests over to see the new baby, make sure they eat or drink something while they are there.

....

Bring a new baby a gift of bread, salt, and an egg, or something silver, which will last longer.

....

Start a baby's life out right by giving a newborn a silver coin.

....

Keep the first clipping of your baby's hair in a safe place— it will provide him with lifelong protection and luck.

DON'T EVER

Knit clothes for future children before you're pregnant.

Buy a baby a gift before it has safely been born.
It is tempting fate and is therefore bad luck.

Measure or weigh a newborn (although it's OK if
your doctor does); it's also seen as tempting fate.

Say how beautiful a baby is, praise him,
or call him a little angel. Again, tempting fate.

Let a baby look in a mirror before she is a year old.

BUYING YOUR FIRST HOME

*Moving into a new home often means a fresh start
and the chance for a new beginning. Here are ways to ensure
that your new home will shelter you with luck.*

....

DEFINITELY WORTH TRYING

If you've built the house, don't forget to have a topping-out ceremony and to add a branch of something green to the highest point of the home when the construction is complete.

....

It's also always good luck to leave the building with something unfinished—even one square inch left unpainted or a minor decorative element that's missing will do the trick.

....

Move to a higher floor in the same apartment building.

....

Move into your new home on a Monday or Wednesday.

Enter the home through the front door, right foot first.

....

Go into every room in your new house with a loaf of bread and a dish of salt—or, better yet, do this with bread and salt that has been given to you as a housewarming gift.

....

Place an acorn on a windowsill or hang it from a window shade.

....

Buy a goldfish.

....

Place the figure of an elephant outside your house, facing your doorway, or hang a horseshoe over the threshold.

DON'T EVER

Move downstairs in the same apartment building.

Move back into a house in which you've already lived.

Move into a new home on a Friday or a Saturday. Friday's just bad luck, and Saturday means a short stay, which would be unfortunate if you've just found the perfect home.

Take an old broom with you when moving into a new house.

First enter a new house through the back door or enter it empty-handed.

Sweep the house you're moving out of—or, if you must, then leave a little something behind. Sweeping away "dirt's luck" is bad luck.

SELLING YOUR HOUSE

When it's time to move on, bury a St. Joseph statue outside your house. This custom has become so prevalent that even realtors subscribe to it. Variations on exact burial specifications exist, so you may want to buy a bunch and try them all, just to be safe. Bury him:

Upside down.

Near the For Sale sign in the front yard.

In the backyard, possibly in a flowerbed.

Lying on his back and pointing toward
the house like an arrow.

Facing the house.

Facing away from the house.

Three feet from the rear of the house.

Exactly twelve inches deep.

RELATIONSHIPS

LOVE, SEX, AND DATING

Get lucky-er.

....

DEFINITELY WORTH TRYING

Guys, head out and get a charm such as a *corno* (horn) or a *palad khik* (honorable surrogate penis) tailor-made to get your groove thing going.

....

Hairy men, you're in luck. Stop waxing your back and luxuriate in the lucky love it will bring.

....

Wear a red ribbon tied in a knot in your hair to catch and keep love.

....

Make sure nothing is knotted in your love nest to ensure successful, ahem, well, you know.

Grab a candle, light it, and stick some pins in it while thinking about the object of your affection; that'll get his or her attention.

....

Get a twig of laurel or bay, break it in half, then keep a piece for yourself and give one to your lover. As long as you have it, your love will thrive.

....

The next time you're out camping, leap over the fire (when there are no flames and only embers); it will bring you luck in love.

Give your lover a key (either real or symbolic) and you will be lucky in love.

....

Kiss someone on New Year's Eve to be kissed all year long.

Although most of us groan at the approach of February 14, don't forget that St. Valentine is the protector of lovers, and this day (Hallmark and red roses aside) is lucky for love.

DON'T EVER

Begin a courtship or even go out on a date on a Friday.

....

Give the gift of a Bible, or a shoe, which encourages the recipient to take a walk.

....

Make a promise by moonlight— it can never be kept.

Give something that is fake (like a cubic zirconia engagement ring), or your love will turn out to be just as phony.

....

Kiss while one of you is seated, or kiss someone while standing behind them. Both are bad luck and bad for your back.

LOVE LETTER

*If you're one to put your thoughts down on paper,
here are a few bits of advice for love-letter writing.*

....

Always write it by hand and in ink
(not in pencil or on the computer).

It's good luck if your hand trembles while you
write it; it means the recipient loves you back.

Don't ever include a proposal in a love letter.

Be sure to put enough postage on the
letter and to seal it thoroughly.
To not do so is to invite bad luck, and the
recipient may think you're cheap.

FRIENDSHIP

You're already lucky if you have good friends,
and here are a few ways to keep them.

....

DEFINITELY WORTH TRYING

Bracelets made of a sequence of knots
(known to trap and keep love) can be given to a
friend as a reinforcement of your emotional ties.

Share a piece of chewing gum (yes, we
mean one person chews it first, then the other)
to ensure that your friendship sticks.

If you and your friend say something at exactly the
same time (which good friends often do), it's good luck,
and you should lock pinkies and each make a wish.

DON'T EVER

Give a friend a knife, scissors, or knitting needles
as a gift; it will cut the ties of the friendship.

Give soap; it doesn't just wash away dirt, but friendship.

Give a friend gloves, unless you want to pick a fight.

PETS

Picking a pet for its propitious properties is potentially problematic.

DOGS 	Although black dogs are often viewed with as much suspicion as black cats and a howling dog is thought to signal death, a strange dog following you on the street or coming into your home is thought to be lucky, as is seeing a spotted dog on the way to a business meeting.
GOLDFISH 	Goldfish are small, domesticated members of the carp family, and if you keep a goldfish you'll be in good company. The Egyptians, Greeks, Chinese, and Japanese have all kept gold-colored fish for hundreds of years, with the belief that they bring good fortune to the home. The most prized gold fish today (particularly in Asia) is the arowana, which is considered to be a money magnet with gills.

FROGS

Although they look silly in bandanas and can't catch Frisbees, frogs make excellent lucky companions. The Romans believed frog charms drew in love and friendship, and many cultures saw a frog entering a home as a harbinger of good fortune. If you have a predilection for gaming, they are also thought to bring good luck in dice games. But be sure you take good care of your little amphibious friend because letting one croak is very bad luck.

CATS

Cats have a pretty bad rap as far as all of this luck business goes. Black ones, white ones, and ones born in May are unlucky. It's unlucky to have them around a baby, to let them walk across a stage, or to even dream about them. Of course, the Egyptians loved them—and the Japanese and sailors' wives think black ones and unfamiliar ones are lucky, while the Indonesians believe calico ones are. Perhaps the luckiest thing about them is that they are thought to have nine lives, although given how unlucky they are, maybe that's not so lucky for us.

SCHOOL AND WORK

SCHOOL AND EXAMS

School days, school days, dear old golden . . . whatever.

DEFINITELY WORTH TRYING

Wear lucky underwear. Try a pair with a superhero insignia, or sew a tag with the score you'd like to receive on your exam into the band of any old pair and wear them on test day.

Eat one strip of bacon and two fried eggs on the morning of an exam. Be sure to arrange them on your plate so they look like the number 100, and your perfect score will follow.

Listen to a song that inspires you. Try "Gonna Fly Now," the theme song to *Rocky*.

Avoid running into a person or passing by a place that has a bad vibe.

Bring a good-luck charm. If you need a new one, try bringing Ganesha, the Hindu god of wisdom and good luck, along with you. A charm or picture of this powerful elephant on your desk or in your pocket will help you successfully surmount any educational obstacle.

Enter the classroom with your right foot first, to ensure you've put your best foot forward.

Use your own lucky ritual. All pre-exam sequences of action—including but not limited to: shaving or not shaving, movie watching, and repeating something you did the last time you did well—are created equal.

....

Circle your desk three times before sitting down for an exam.

Sit in your favorite or usual seat.

....

Exchange Kit Kats with fellow test takers. In Japanese, the words *Kit Kat* sound like *kitto katsu*, which roughly translate to "I hope you will win."

....

Lucky #2. Be sure to use a favorite pencil (or pen).

DON'T EVER

Sing before breakfast on the morning of an exam—you won't do well.

Drop your books on your way to class, since it means you'll make a mistake while there.

Stare at the teacher's back (unless you know the answer to the question); it will make her more likely to call on you.

CYBERLUCK

It's important that everything you do on the computer, whether it's working, chatting, gambling, gaming, or shopping, be wired for luck. And although the regular rules still apply (if you're playing online blackjack, make sure you're wearing red underwear), there are some extra things you can do to ensure e-Luck.

....

DEFINITELY WORTH TRYING

Save your computer's memory with a USB Mamory charm (a play on the Japanese *omamori* good-luck charm and the word *memory*), which was created to bring good IT luck.

....

Create a screensaver that allows you to virtually knock on wood whenever you might need to.

....

Although mice are generally considered unlucky, make your computer mouse a lucky mascot by giving him a name or ears.

Choose a lucky color as your desktop default.

....

Have the character you control in a video game perform a lucky ritual (jumping, hopping, circling, whatever) before beginning an important or dangerous action.

....

Perform an animal sacrifice to appease the electronic luck gods. Download the image of a goat or cow and then delete it from your computer.

DON'T EVER

Tempt fate by boasting of your problem-free computing
or by not saving documents regularly.

Forward an e-mail (or snail mail, for that matter)
chain letter, especially if it's asking for money. Set up like Ponzi
schemes, these letters extort susceptible recipients with
threats of bad luck. Remember, luck doesn't answer to blackmail.

Hack. It's the virtual equivalent of entering a building
through the back door, which is always unlucky.

Type a love letter on the computer; any important sentiment
should be expressed by hand and in ink.

AT THE OFFICE

*Whether you're just starting out in the mailroom and
need a leg up or you've already commandeered the corner
office and just want to hold onto it, you can enhance your
career luck by incorporating these rules into your work life.*

....

DEFINITELY WORTH TRYING

If you have to make a tough
professional decision, do it on
a Thursday.

....

A golden pig placed on your
desk will ensure the dedication
of your employees. And an image of a phoenix will kick-start
company initiatives.

....

Avoid sitting in line with a door
or a long corridor that can drain
away good luck.

....

It's no good (and it totally sucks)
to have a view of storage closets
or toilets, which are rife with
bad luck.

Answer your phone; it's bad luck
(and business) to let a ringing
one go unanswered. It's also
bad luck if you answer it and no
one's there, but there's not much
you can do about that.

....

Wear your lucky outfit, use
your lucky pen, and drink out
of your lucky mug when you
have an important meeting or
presentation.

....

If you share an office with
someone, try to arrange your
desks so that you sit side by
side, to ensure luck will flow
between you.

Sit facing the entrance to your office with your back toward a wall—the position of "command." Or, at least never have your back to the door.

....

Always have your favorite lucky charm close at hand.

Bring some lucky greenery into your office, like a jade plant or a money tree, or buy a kit to grow your own four-leaf clovers; it's not as lucky as finding one of them by chance outdoors, but who has time to look for one when you're always at the office?

DON'T EVER

Tempt fate by discussing the end of a project, a promotion, or a raise before it has happened.

....

Wear an item of clothing you wore during a failed presentation or when you were fired.

....

Let clutter build up, as it blocks the flow of good luck.

Wear green or use it in a logo, letterhead, or the packaging of an important product; it's an inauspicious color.

....

Let broken or malfunctioning items go unattended, and plumbing tops the list. The last thing you need is your cash flow backed up.

BUSINESS

What does Donald Trump have besides really strange hair?
Good luck in business! Whether buying or selling or convincing
someone else to buy or sell, everyone can use that extra edge.

DEFINITELY WORTH TRYING

Be careful when choosing a name for a new enterprise; a bad name will mean bad business.

Sign a long-term lease (for an odd number of years); it makes it easier for the money to find you.

Start your new business to coincide with the new moon.

Pick a mascot. It can be an object, person, or animal. Whether it's a favorite shirt, your uncle Fred, or a Chihuahua, this companion is sure to bring good fortune, as long as all of your transactions are aboveboard.

Keep any (or all) of your favorite charms (rabbit's foot, four-leaf clover, etc.) close at hand.

Present friends with a lucky horseshoe of flowers the day their business opens.

Buy a St. Homobonus statuette. Don't forget, he's the patron saint of businesspeople.

After you've sold something, give the buyer back some small amount of money in return. This is called "luck money" and is sure to add luck to the transaction.

A Maneki Neko (Beckoning Cat) good-luck statue placed in the window of your place of business will attract customers and money.

....

Place a piece of malachite, bloodstone, or citrine in the cash register; all three will attract more money.

....

Take note of when you make your first sale of the week. If it's before 9:00 a.m. on Monday, you're in good shape for the rest of the week.

....

Cough or blow on the first money you receive to be sure it doesn't carry bad luck with it. And then kiss or spit on it so it brings more.

Wipe the money you're about to give out as change on the first sale of the week to prevent the good luck from leaving with it.

....

Shake hands or have a drink at the completion of a transaction. It symbolizes unity of purpose and mutual good fortune.

....

Pay attention to who you see when you're out on business. If you meet the same person twice, it's good luck. If you encounter the same person when you are setting out and then again when you are returning, it's even better.

....

"Sell in May and go away" goes an old stock-market saying. And just think, then you'll have the summer off.

DON'T EVER

Make dishonorable transactions. It's likely to fall under the disapproval of the guardians overseeing your mascot and sure to bring loss, accidents, or other business misfortune.

Move your place of business year after year—it makes it harder for the money to find you.

Sign a contract on a Friday— or, worse yet, on Friday the thirteenth.

Botch the first transaction of a day—it's likely to ruin your chances of others.

Overly praise an item you're trying to sell. It's sure to bring bad luck.

THE SHOWDOWN

Although you may think showdowns are a thing of the past, today's competitive work environment proves that they don't just happen at the movies, but in offices, courtrooms, and on the trading floor.

DEFINITELY WORTH TRYING

Slaughter a hog before you slaughter the enemy; have bacon for breakfast or a BLT for lunch in preparation for the event.

Sprinkle cinnamon on your cappuccino—you'll be wide awake and warmed up for any necessary verbal gymnastics.

Choose a lucky day for any important negotiation. Try a Tuesday, which is a proven day for confrontations and competition, or a Wednesday, which is the luckiest day of the week.

Play Beethoven's Fifth (Vth) Symphony before heading out. Why? The Morse code for *v* is three dots and a dash, and the music should put you in a victorious frame of mind.

Appropriate the *v*, for *victory*, as your personal symbol of triumph, and write it on your favorite underwear.

If classical's not your thing, try the theme song to *Rocky*, and picture yourself running up those stairs in Philadelphia.

DON'T EVER

Wear green. It's an unfavorable color for any important dealings and suggests you don't know what you're doing.

Shake hands across a table or desk or ever shake with your left hand.

Sit with your back to the door; it's unlucky and leaves you vulnerable to attack.

LEISURE

IN THE CASINO

Beginner's luck is always guaranteed when you first step into a casino, but after your first time, it may take some of these added measures to keep the luck rolling.

....

DEFINITELY WORTH TRYING

Switch on all the lights at home (or in your hotel room) before going out to gamble.

....

Wear red underwear while you're playing.

....

Wear a dirty item of clothing (particularly when you're playing poker).

....

Carry dice in your pocket.

....

Wear a horn, or *corno*, charm around your neck, or, really, carry any sort of good luck charm that works for you.

Carry a piece of aventurine, cat's-eye, jade, or a mojo bag to attract luck.

....

Stroke the hump of a hunchback before gambling. Although it's not always practical to have a hunchback sidekick, it is possible to purchase a *gobbo* (hunchback) charm and rub it before picking a card or rolling the dice.

....

If things are getting stale, change your seat or go to the washroom and relieve yourself to change your luck.

"Back your luck"—keep at it if you're having a lucky streak.

Blow on the dice, snap your fingers, or rub the dice on a redheaded person before throwing them.

Break bad luck by sitting on a handkerchief, or any other kind of square.

Turn the back of your chair to the table and sit astride it.

Walk around your gaming table three times, clockwise.

"He who borrows money to play will win, but he who lends money to play will lose"—so hit up your friends for money to play with.

DON'T EVER

Let a woman touch you on the shoulder while you're playing (they're always looking for someone to blame, aren't they?).

Gamble with a two-dollar bill.

Bet on a horse that's changed its name.

Count your money while you're still playing.

Lend someone else money to play with while you're playing.

Play angry or for money before 6:00 p.m. on Friday.

Place a matchstick across one that is already in an ashtray.

Mention "books" while gambling. The word in Chinese sounds like the word for "lose."

CARDS

All of the rules of luck that apply in the casino also work with cards,
but here are just a few more lucky tricks to keep up your sleeve.

....

DEFINITELY WORTH TRYING

Stand up and rotate your chair clockwise three times on one of its front legs.

....

Blow or cough on your cards or hands before starting to play.

....

Wear a crooked pin on your coat or shirt.

....

Sit cross-legged.

....

Keep score with a red pencil.

If you're sitting at a wooden table, try to pick a spot facing in the direction of the wood grain—it'll help the luck flow.

....

Even if you're left-handed, pick up your cards with your right hand.

....

Though hard to procure, both a hangman's rope and a badger's tooth are known good-luck charms for card players.

 DON'T EVER

Allow a person to stand over you and look at your cards.

Drop a card during a game.

Whistle or sing while your partner is playing.

CRAPS

*Craps players are among the most superstitious gamblers
and although many have personal, idiosyncratic lucky rituals,
following are the most universally recognized.*

....

DEFINITELY WORTH TRYING

Although it may be difficult to orchestrate, meeting a frog in the road on the way to a dice game is sure to bring luck.

....

Blow on the dice before you shoot them to warm them up.

If you're shooting, stand on one foot until the roll is over.

....

Ask for the number you need when the dice are in mid-air; it can influence the outcome of the roll.

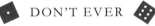 DON'T EVER

Look the shooter in the eye while he has the dice; it will cause him to seven out. If you do, look him in the eye a second time to reverse your mistake.

....

Mention the number seven after the come out roll.

Put money down for chips in the middle of a roll since the boxman and dealers will then have to stop between tosses to set the new player up. This will unfortunately result in the dice getting cold and losing their lucky momentum.

SPORTS

Some lucky things are true for playing all sports.

....

DEFINITELY WORTH TRYING

Run into a wedding on your way to a game.

....

Show up to a match or bout after your opponent; it's luckier than arriving first.

....

Put on your right sneaker, cleat, or ice skate before the left when getting dressed for a game.

....

Kick the goal post three times before the game starts.

....

Eat the exact same meal before every game.

Bounce the ball three times in the center of the field or court before playing.

....

Pass the ball from the oldest player to the youngest player before the match. The youngest must catch the ball on the bounce for good luck.

....

When engaging in dangerous sports (which doesn't mean driving your golf cart quickly but might mean skydiving or spelunking), wear turquoise (the stone or the color) for protection.

DON'T EVER

Have sex before a big game.

Cross the path of a funeral on the way to a game.

SMELLS LIKE TEAM SPIRIT

If you do it, they will win.

DEFINITELY WORTH TRYING

Wear team colors on game day.

If your team wins, don't shave your facial hair. If your team loses, shave your facial hair.*

If it's working, don't change it. This includes a cap, T-shirt, underwear, or socks that you were wearing when your team won.

Cheer to shoo away bad luck.

Yell at the television; it helps.

Turn your cap around or inside out to reverse your team's luck.*

Park it in the same place—be it your car in the lot or your butt on the couch—before the game.

DON'T EVER

Jinx a player by talking about his stats, say "no-hitter" about a pitcher, or talk about the outcome of a game before it's over.*

Put your baseball cap on a bed.*

Fill in a scorecard before a play or player is entirely done.*

Wear your opponent's team color on game day (or on any day, for that matter).

These also apply if you're playing a sport as well as just watching it.

BASEBALL

Playing baseball affords the perfect opportunity to create your own lucky rituals. But if you're looking for some surefire things to do and avoid, here are a few of the tried-and-true.

....

DEFINITELY WORTH TRYING

Kick the mound or the plate before each pitch or at bat.

....

Love the bat, talk to the bat, sleep with the bat.

....

Tap your bat on home plate before batting.

....

Use your lucky number as your uniform number.

Spit on your hands before batting or in your glove before pitching or fielding.

....

Turn your cap around backward to reverse the direction of your (or your team's) luck.

....

Tap your toes with the bat and adjust your batting gloves before you step in.

DON'T EVER

Let two bats cross on the baseball field.

Switch bats after a second strike.

Step on the foul line.

GOLF

Here are some handicaps that are actually lucky.

....

DEFINITELY WORTH TRYING

Carry an old lucky club with you in your bag—even if you don't use it anymore.

....

Tee off with a ball that has the lowest odd number possible (except the number three)— the higher the number, the higher the score.

....

Discard a bogey ball.

Take extra care when playing the thirteenth hole.

....

Use a lucky coin (head side up) to mark your ball on the green.

....

Carry a St. Andrew medal with you. He's the patron saint of Scotland (the birthplace of golf) and, many say, of golfers in particular.

DON'T EVER

Tee off with a number-three ball, which might lend itself to a three-putt and possibly a bogey.

....

Clean a ball when the game is going your way.

Say the word *shank*, which is the unluckiest part of the club a golfer can hit a ball with.

....

Change a club once you have selected it.

TENNIS

*Whether at Wimbledon, Roland-Garros, or 119th Street
and Riverside Drive, it's always a good idea to court luck.*

....

DEFINITELY WORTH TRYING

Tap your tennis racket on your feet for luck,
or bounce the ball on your racket a prescribed
number of times before serving.

Avoid stepping on the lines between points.

Spit on your hands before serving or playing
an important point.

Bounce the ball three times (or however many
times feels right) before serving.

DON'T EVER

Serve while holding three balls, and don't serve
with a ball that you just faulted with.

Let a ball drop out of your pocket;
the luck spills out with it. Besides, if it happens
twice, you'll lose the point, which
has nothing to do with luck, it's just the rule.

GONE FISHIN'

These tips will come in handy when you're angling for luck.

....

DEFINITELY WORTH TRYING

Spit on your bait before casting.

....

Place a lucky coin on your float.

....

Throw back your first catch.

If the fish just aren't biting, do as the Scottish do and push a fellow fisherman into the water, then haul him back as if he were a fish.

DON'T EVER

Bait a hook with your left hand.

....

Let anyone walk over your line. It should always be lifted and walked under.

....

Change rods in the middle of a day of fishing.

....

Throw away a float that has worked for you in the past.

....

Sit on an upturned bucket.

Let your net touch the water before the fish has taken the bait (it's tempting fate).

....

Count your fish before you're done for the day.

....

Ask other fishermen how many bites they've had.

....

Brag about how many fish you have caught in the past or how big they were.

LUCKY DUCK

OK, ducks really aren't lucky at all,
but there are birds that are.

....

DEFINITELY WORTH TRYING

Although difficult to choreograph intentionally,
it is lucky if bird droppings fall on you.

Grab your binoculars and search for a
cuckoo, lark, martin, nightingale, robin, swallow,
or wren. They're all lucky birds to see.

Buy a canary. They are thought to bring
happiness and luck to any home.

DON'T EVER

Although it's hard to imagine you would, don't allow a cat to eat your canary; it's bad luck for two years.

Harm the nest of a lark, martin, robin, swallow, or wren.

Injure an albatross, lark, martin, robin, swallow, or wren.

Allow a bird to tap on your window—especially not a robin. It's a sign of imminent death.

Trap a wild bird inside your home, particularly not a robin. This is apparently such bad luck that many believe you shouldn't even have wallpaper, pictures, or any decorative items with birds on them in your home.

Bring the eggs of wild birds or peacock feathers inside your home.

Go looking for a blackbird, crow, jackdaw, a single magpie (if you see two or more, you're spared), owl (hooting after nightfall), peacock, pigeon, raven, rook, sparrow, swift, whippoorwill, or yellowhammer. Spotting any of them is considered unlucky.

Seek out a dead bird (we suppose this doesn't include ones in the poultry section of the grocery store). You should spit on the body of any one you happen to find to avert the bad luck that comes from having spotted it.

SEWING

They say a stitch in time saves nine, but who really cares?
The question is, Will it bring you luck?

....

DEFINITELY WORTH TRYING

As frustrating as it is, tangling thread while sewing is good luck.

....

To give a thimble as a gift is lucky for the recipient.

....

Dropping a sewing needle while sewing is good luck.

To lose a thimble is to bring good luck to the person you're sewing for, although if you're sewing something for yourself only time will tell if it was worth the effort of having to go find a new one.

DON'T EVER

Use dark- or black-colored thread while mending a light-colored garment; it's bad luck as well as poor workmanship.

....

Sew on a Sunday or begin a new project on a Friday.

Drop your scissors while sewing. If you do, step on them to avert bad luck.

....

Sew or mend an item of clothing while it is being worn by you or another person.

KNITTING

Casting around for lucky ideas? Here are a few to consider.

....

DEFINITELY WORTH TRYING

Always cast on a new project immediately after finishing
one; knitting needles should never be left empty.

Knit a boyfriend (or girlfriend) socks for a
present if you want to subtly get rid of him. Like the
gift of shoes, it will invite him to "take a walk."

DON'T EVER

Stop knitting when you're only on the cast-on row;
it means the project will never be completed.

Although it's OK to begin knitting or sewing a gift for
a baby before it is born, do not tell the parents about the gift
or give it to them before the baby has been safely delivered.

Knit in a theater—either on stage or in the wings.

Knit a boyfriend (or girlfriend) a sweater for a present if you
want to keep him (or her). Doing so simply tempts fate.

Give knitting needles as a gift—
they will weaken the ties of the relationship.

SHOPPING

*Shopping is not just an opportunity to get new stuff; it's a
chance to get new stuff* and *bring more luck into your life.*

....

DEFINITELY WORTH TRYING

Subtly suggest the item you want
to purchase is somehow faulty or
damaged. Be sure when you do
so that you also say something to
show you don't mean any harm.
An example: "That hideous old
sweater? I might be willing to
take it off your hands." It's good
bargaining and good luck.

....

Wear a pair of crossed pins
somewhere on your person—
you'll be sure to get better deals.

....

Always guarantee the luck
(or "handsel") of a new item
of clothing you purchase by
putting a coin in the pocket
or seam.

Be sure to accept "luck money"
that has been offered back to
you by a seller. This could include taking something offered
to you outright, such as a rebate,
or grabbing a coin from the
"take a penny, leave a penny"
container that many merchants
have near their cash registers.
It's lucky for both of you.

....

Leave a deposit on something
you want to purchase later.
Called "God's penny," a deposit
made on a purchase once served
as a promise that the transaction
would be made in full at a later
date and, as a token of goodwill,
brought luck along with it.

DON'T EVER

Buy a broom in May or at Christmastime.

Tempt fate by buying something until it's
absolutely needed. This goes double for baby gifts,
including cradles, strollers, and clothes.

Buy eggs after sundown.

Buy a pair of squeaky shoes. Noisy shoes are said to be
stolen, and people will think you haven't paid for them.

Buy anything with a two-dollar bill.

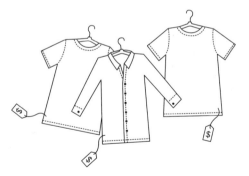

THE GIFT OF LUCK

*Some things are particularly lucky (or unlucky) to give
or receive as gifts. Here is a list of things to be on the lookout
for or to avoid when shopping for special occasions.*

DEFINITELY WORTH BUYING

Although in the eighteenth and nineteenth centuries it was considered good luck to bring a newborn baby bread, salt, and an egg, most people today prefer bringing a silver—and equally auspicious—gift.

Anything you give (especially an item of clothing, purse, or wallet) can be made lucky, or "handseled," with the inclusion of a penny or other coin and is sure to bring luck to the recipient.

Give a bride a pot of honey for luck.

Never go to a new house empty-handed; bring a gift, however small. Salt, a new broom, and even a lump of coal are all excellent choices.

A glass rolling pin is another lucky gift for an engagement or wedding.

Give a friend a bouquet of jasmine and gardenias—it'll strengthen the bonds of your friendship.

Wrapping any gift with a red ribbon is sure to invest it with lucky qualities.

For wedding anniversaries, any gift made of the following material for the corresponding anniversary is considered lucky.

FIRST	01	PAPER
FIFTH	05	WOOD
TENTH	10	TIN OR ALUMINUM
FIFTEENTH	15	CRYSTAL
TWENTIETH	20	CHINA
TWENTY-FIFTH	25	SILVER
THIRTIETH	30	PEARL
THIRTY-FIFTH	35	CORAL
FORTIETH	40	RUBY
FORTY-FIFTH	45	SAPPHIRE
FIFTIETH	50	GOLD
FIFTY-FIFTH	55	EMERALD
SIXTIETH	60	DIAMOND
SEVENTY-FIFTH	75	DIAMOND

DON'T EVER GIVE

Bellows, to a wedding couple. They're probably not on the Crate & Barrel registry anyway.

Bath salts or soap; they will wash away friendship.

A handkerchief, which is said to be like giving the gift of tears. And who wants that?

A Bible. This is extra bad for a boyfriend to give his girlfriend (and talk about not romantic).

Gloves. Giving them is likely to cause an argument or, more seriously, jeopardize a friendship.

Umbrellas; they are considered unlucky gifts (as well as boring).

A clock. For the Chinese, it literally suggests, "I am waiting for you to die."

Shoes. Although Imelda Marcos would be sad to hear it.

Sharp objects such as knives, scissors, or even pins, which are thought to "cut" the ties of the relationship.

Red and white flowers in a bouquet. And never to someone recovering from an illness.

ANTIDOTE

The best way to undo the damage if someone unknowingly gives you one of these unlucky gifts is to give them a penny or another coin in return. The gift is then technically considered a purchase and not subject to the same unlucky laws.

TRAVELING

Whether you're on the road, in the air, or out to sea,
here are some measures that may help ensure that your
bon voyage doesn't become a bum voyage.

....

DEFINITELY WORTH TRYING

Knock on wood when you mention your destination.

....

Sit on your suitcase before your departure to ensure happy trails.

....

Always leave your home and enter a new place with your right foot first.

....

If you happen to see a snail on your way out, pick it up and toss it (lightly) over your left shoulder, to prevent a sluggish start to your travels.

....

Carry a St. Christopher medal with you. He is, after all, the patron saint of travelers.

Although we don't suggest trying this at JFK International Airport, relieving yourself on the wheels of a plane is said to guarantee a safe flight.

....

Pick a flight that has an auspicious number (777, for example) or that corresponds to your lucky number.

....

If the spot next to you on an airplane is empty, cross the unused seatbelts for a safe flight.

....

If you're considering taking Fluffy along on your cruise to the Caribbean, go for it. Cats on boats are good luck.

Turquoise is a known good-luck stone for aviators, so, pilot or passenger, wearing it while flying is sure to bring good luck.

Throw an old shoe after someone embarking on a long trip.

Bring along a *kaeru* frog on your travels. In Japanese *kaeru* means both "frog" and "to return," and putting this little charm into your carry-on luggage will ensure you arrive back home safely.

DON'T EVER

Start a trip on a Friday—or, worse, on Friday the thirteenth.

Stumble when leaving for your trip. If you do, you might consider postponing.

Look back when leaving a loved one behind.

Turn back to get something that you have forgotten or return to your house once you've started off on your trip.

Mention the words *delay, emergency landing,* or *crash* when discussing a plane trip.

Whistle on a boat; it's likely to bring on dangerous gales.

Take a hotel room with an inauspicious number or on the thirteenth floor.

Give white flowers (and certainly not white and red flowers) to someone leaving on a trip.

SO JUST WHO WAS
ST. CHRISTOPHER, ANYWAY?

Although millions of people refuse to take a trip without a St. Christopher medal or token with them, very few people know who St. Christopher was or how he came to be associated with traveling. There are several legends about him, including one where he, originally named Offero, was enlisted by a hermit to carry travelers across a river for money. One night he began to carry a child across and, as they got farther and farther into the river, the child became heavier and heavier. The child revealed himself as Jesus Christ, who was so heavy because he was bearing the weight of the world. Forced down into the water because of the burden, Offero was thus baptized and given the name Christopher, meaning "Christ-bearer." He was later martyred and has since become the popular subject of early Christian art and the patron saint of travelers. The feast of St. Christopher is celebrated on July 25.

CAR

Since geckos are not actually considered lucky,
here are some things you can do to ensure a smooth ride.

....

DEFINITELY WORTH TRYING

Bring St. Frances of Rome along for a ride (particularly at night) or St. Christopher.

....

Hang a horn, or *corno,* good-luck charm or a pair of lucky dice from your rearview mirror if you plan to drive at fast speeds.

....

If you're buying a new car, bring along any charms from your old car if it's been a lucky one.

Pick a taxi with a horseshoe-like *U* in the license plate number.

....

Pick your feet up off the floor and touch the roof of the car when going over railroad tracks or when passing a cemetery.

....

Kiss your hand and touch the roof of the car if you run a red light (although we're sure it was really yellow, too).

DON'T EVER

Rent or buy a green car.

Accept a license plate that includes the number thirteen.

Boast about what great time you made on your last
car trip or talk about how little traffic there is.

CELEBRATIONS

YOU SAY IT'S YOUR BIRTHDAY

Since you have to get older, why not also get luckier?

....

DEFINITELY WORTH TRYING

Have a birthday cake, complete with a candle that represents each year you've been around and an extra one for luck.

....

Let someone give you a spank (lightly!) for each year you've been alive, and an extra for luck.

Make a silent wish while blowing out the candles.

....

Blow all of the candles out in one breath.

....

Have a meal of long noodles to ensure a long life.

DON'T EVER

Leave any of the candles on your birthday cake lit.

....

Cry on your birthday; it means you'll cry the rest of the year.

....

Tell anyone your wish; it won't come true.

Tell your real age. If someone asks and you must tell, either add or subtract a year to avoid tempting the same sneaky fates who are waiting for you to count your money at the gambling table or talk about all the fish you've caught.

NEW YEAR, LUCKY YOU

The best way to guarantee luck in the future is to start the year off right.

DEFINITELY WORTH TRYING

Wear something new; it maximizes your chances of getting more new clothes in the upcoming year.

Open the front door just before midnight; it will help let in the New Year.

It's always a good idea to make noise at the toll of midnight on New Year's Eve; it not only shoos away the evil spirits from the old year but also provides fresh air for the new.

Having the last drink from a bottle on New Year's Eve is good luck. And is likely to encourage you to do more . . .

Kissing! Puckering up at the stroke of midnight means you'll be smooching all year long.

The "first foot" is an important part of the New Year's tradition and refers to the first person who crosses your threshold after midnight. Lucky custom dictates he should be a dark man who is, hopefully, bringing a gift of bread, a lump of coal, salt, or money, all of which will guarantee a prosperous year. Once you've let him in, let him out the back so he takes the old year out with him. If you live in an apartment, let him do a circuit around the place and then let him back out the front.

The first Monday of the New Year is particularly auspicious, and you should be sure to invest it with luck (or "handsel" it) to ensure a fruitful year by giving or getting money (either as charity or as part of a business transaction) on that day.

DON'T EVER

Hang a new calendar before the old year is out;
it's tempting fate.

Let a blond, redhead, or (gasp!) woman
(especially a widow) be your first-footer; it's bad luck.

Leave your cupboards or pockets empty on New Year's Eve;
it means they will stay bare for the rest of the year.

Let the fire in a fireplace go out on New Year's Eve.
If you're worried about safety (or don't have a fireplace),
keep a light burning instead.

Wash your clothes on New Year's Day; it's said
to mean a death in the family.

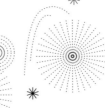

WELLNESS

BEAUTY

Well, we're not all lucky enough to be born with
a face that can launch a thousand ships.

....

DEFINITELY WORTH TRYING

For luck in looks, gather the dew off the grass on the first of May and bathe in it. Canyon Ranch might already offer this service.

....

Wear red lipstick; it'll help you retain the good luck you have.

....

Wear mascara or black eyeliner, as the Egyptians did, to protect you from the evil eye.

Get your nails done to display prominent half-moons, which are considered lucky.

....

Don't feel bad if your nails have white spots—they are considered "good-luck spots."

....

Get a haircut or manicure on Tuesday, Wednesday, Thursday, Saturday, or, better yet, Monday.

DON'T EVER

Get your hair or nails cut on Friday or Sunday.

Spill face powder or any loose makeup.

SMOKING

If you're a smoker, you're definitely going to need some good luck.

....

DEFINITELY WORTH TRYING

Flip one cigarette over when you open a fresh pack of cigarettes, and smoke that "lucky" one last.

....

If you are passing a cigarette, be sure you pass it clockwise.

....

Blow a smoke ring and put your finger through the center while making a wish.

If you happen to be subjected to someone else's smoke, you can do the same thing to their smoke ring.

....

Read your romantic future in your cigarette. A cigarette that keeps going out is a sure sign that you are in love (and that it is not in vain).

DON'T EVER

Take the third light off a match.

....

Offer or accept a broken cigar.

....

Relight a cigarette three times.

....

Light a pipe from a candle or the fire from a fireplace.

Light a cigar off someone else's.

....

Use the last match in a matchbook.

....

Let your cigar or cigarette burn unevenly on one side; it's a sure sign of trouble.

HEALTH AND HOSPITALS

*Although nothing can replace good medical
insurance coupled with a knowledgeable health-care worker,
here are a few things your HMO might not know.*

....

DEFINITELY WORTH TRYING

If you see an ambulance, hold your breath and pinch your nose until it's gone; it's good luck for the passenger.

....

If someone has given you a bouquet of flowers during a hospital stay, leave them (and your illness) behind when you are discharged.

....

Try selling your health problem to a friend. Offer to give her a good deal—say, a buck fifty—on your tendonitis. Some believe that the evil spirits that control the illness will get confused as to who should actually have it and the problem will go away.

It's good luck if you stay in a hospital bed where the person before you had an easy recovery.

....

"An apple a day keeps the doctor away." It's sort of an old, tired saying, but it just may work.

....

For physical therapy, take a stroll in a clockwise direction.

....

If you're having an elective procedure, try to get admitted on a Wednesday*—it's the luckiest day to begin a medical treatment. Do not do this if you have a medical *emergency;* there's nothing lucky about waiting too long for needed treatment.

DON'T EVER

Leave a hospital on a Saturday* if you can help it;
it means you will be back.

Say you're "very well" or "feeling great"
when asked how you are doing; it's tempting fate.

Accept white or red and white flowers while sick.

Pay a doctor's bill in full. Although the doctor
won't like to hear this, it's considered to be tempting
fate to act as though your treatment is over.

....

*In Japan, studies have shown that the belief in taian (lucky day) and
butsumetsu (unlucky day) among hospital patients is high, and a disproportionate
number of patients are released on taian, but very few on butsumetsu.

DEATH

Well, OK, dying isn't such a lucky thing, but many believe there are ways to make the transition from this life to the afterlife luckier for both the unfortunate loved one and for those left behind.

DEFINITELY WORTH TRYING

Mirrors should be covered after someone dies. This is both a sign of respect (vanity should not be present when a loved one has died) and a way to be sure the soul of the dead does not become distracted and stay behind. Alternatively, mirrors can also be turned toward the wall.

Some suggest that touching a corpse brings luck.

Doors and windows should be kept unlocked or open to provide an easy path of departure. Many extend this practice to drawers and cupboards as well.

Funeral processions should always approach a graveyard clockwise and should never be pointed at, for fear of bad luck.

Buy and burn paper effigies of everything your dearly departed might need in the afterlife during the Chinese Hungry Ghost Festival (fourteenth night of the seventh lunar month). Although traditionally only fake money was burned, today paper replicas of everything from Mercedes-Benzes and laptop computers to call girls and Viagra can be purchased to make death a little more pleasurable.

DON'T EVER

Stand at the foot of the bed when someone dies. It might prevent that person's soul from easily passing.

....

Knots are likewise thought to cause obstructions and should not be found anywhere on the dying person's clothing or shoes.

....

Wear mourning clothes beyond one year—it invites tragedy.

Although expectant heirs might hate us for this, it's unlucky to make a will, as some see it as hurrying the inevitable.

....

Speak ill of the dead, which might summon them to defend themselves against the insult.

....

Let a dog or cat near a body— and it is bad luck to encounter either on the way to a gravesite.

IN CASE OF EMERGENCY

You're likely to slip up every once in a while and do something that's unlucky. Or maybe you're just having a terrible day. Here's a list of things you can do to try to undo what's been done or to turn your luck around quickly.

SPITTING 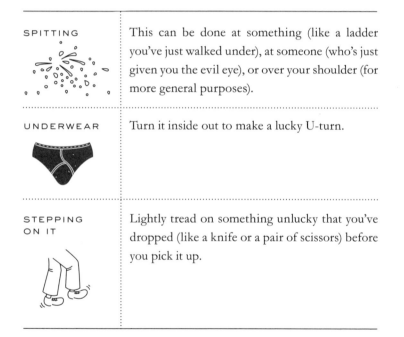	This can be done at something (like a ladder you've just walked under), at someone (who's just given you the evil eye), or over your shoulder (for more general purposes).
UNDERWEAR	Turn it inside out to make a lucky U-turn.
STEPPING ON IT	Lightly tread on something unlucky that you've dropped (like a knife or a pair of scissors) before you pick it up.

CROSSING	Cross your fingers, your legs, or yourself to ward off bad luck.
CLOCKWISE MOTION	Turn in place or circle an object three times clockwise.
KNOCKING ON WOOD	To ward off tempted fate. If you can't find real wood, knock on your head, on paper (that was wood at some point in its life), or on this book.
HAND JIVE	Use the *mano cornuto* (stick out your little finger and your index finger while touching your thumb and other fingers to you palm) or the *mano fico* (make a fist while sticking your thumb between your middle and index fingers) to repel any bad luck heading your way.

C	O	R	N	O	P	L	E
L	G	E	T	S	I	U	H
H	N	E	E	R	G	C	G
U	M	B	R	E	L	L	A
N							L
C							U
H							C
B							K
A	F	R	O	G	I	N	Y
C	B	O	L	U	C	K	H
K	B	G	O	B	B	O	X
R	E	D	C	F	E	Y	P

It's time for you to take control of your own luck. And here are all the tools you'll need—charts, diagrams, and worksheets—to identify and get the most out of the luck in your life. Remember, none of these things will work unless you try them out, so roll up your sleeves and get lucky!

GET LUCKIER NOW

If you've ever wondered why some people are luckier than others, you're already off on the wrong track. The consensus among sociologists, behavioral psychologists, and other experts who have studied the phenomenon of luck is that lucky people aren't born—they're made. Creating your own luck really is possible, and it all comes down to five essential rules.

....

BE OPEN TO EVERYTHING AND EVERYONE. Although your parents warned you not to, you should talk to strangers. And you should talk to them as much as possible, wherever you can. Studies have shown that the most successful people are the ones who take the trouble to form friendly contacts at any opportunity. So the next time you're in the supermarket checkout line, talk to the person next to you. Really. It's got to be more edifying than reading about that boy who got trapped in a freezer and ate his own foot.

BELIEVE YOU ARE LUCKY. If you expect good things to happen to you, they will. And if you believe you are a lucky person, you will be. Psychologists say that people who don't feel lucky tend to stick with the program and do the same things over and over, even if they're unhappy. On the other hand, people who do feel lucky are more likely to take risks and try something new. They are more likely to enter into a new business venture, a new relationship, or even a contest. And as they say, you can't win if you don't play. So start thinking of yourself as the lucky person you already are.

TRUST YOUR HUNCHES. As sentient beings, we're not able to process all of the sensory data we are bombarded with each second on a conscious level. But we are on a subconscious level. And hunches are actually based on the information that we absorb and process while we're doing other things. That's why hunches feel the way they do—you don't quite know why you feel a certain way about something, but you just do. So pay attention to and trust your gut when making decisions. Chances are, it's right.

SHAKE THINGS UP. If you're stuck in a routine, doing the same things every single day, you're likely missing out on lucky experiences that can only come from exposure. So go to more parties, or try out that new restaurant. Try sitting with people you don't know at lunch or reconnecting with old friends. Take a class, a different route to work, or a break, even if you don't need one. Take a shower at a random time, since that's when the best ideas often occur. If you are open to exploring new places and experiences, sooner or later you're bound to find yourself at the right place at the right time.

BE PREPARED FOR LUCK. OK, the Boy Scouts were right about this. It's one thing to be in the right place at the right time; it's another altogether to know what to do when your lucky number gets called. Lucky opportunities always present themselves at the most unexpected times (that's why they're lucky), and you've got to be prepared to notice when one is happening and take advantage of it. So pay attention to your surroundings at all times—that way when your big lucky break comes along, you'll be ready.

WEEKLY LUCK PLANNER

There are certain days of the week when it's luckier
(or unluckier) than others to engage in certain activities.
If you like to plan ahead, here are the guidelines.

MONDAY

is the best day to announce an ambitious project or begin a large-scale undertaking. It's a lucky day to receive money if you own a business, and a good day not to spend any yourself. It's also a good day to have a visitor, to do laundry, and the best day to get a haircut and manicure.

TUESDAY

is a good day to work in the garden, although be careful on Tuesdays with sharp objects. You might find yourself or others argumentative on Tuesdays, so it may be a good day to engage in business negotiations or legal transactions if that will give you an edge. This is a good day for a haircut and manicure, although it's a bad day to meet a left-handed person.

WEDNESDAY

is the luckiest day overall. It is the best day for correspondences, so if you have a thank-you note to write or e-mails to catch up on, today's the day to tackle them. Wednesday is a good day for a haircut and manicure but not a good day for big purchases.

THURSDAY

is the best day to make a big decision or perform a difficult task. It's a good day for a haircut and manicure.

FRIDAY

is the unluckiest day of the week, especially when it falls on the thirteenth of the month. It's a bad day for mattress or feather-bed turning or for changing your sheets, doing laundry, putting on clean clothes, or getting a haircut or manicure. Never begin anything new on a Friday, including a job, a project, a trip, a relationship, or even a box of cereal. And try not to get sick on a Friday.

SATURDAY

mornings should be spent telling your bed partner what you dreamt about Friday night; if it was a good dream and you tell about it, it will come true. You shouldn't work on Saturday or begin a new project, although it's a good day for a haircut and manicure. It's the worst day to do laundry, with implications that reach far beyond what might be rationally expected: "Wash on Friday, wash in need; wash on Saturday, a slut indeed." Harsh, right?

SUNDAY

is the best day to do nothing. Expressly prohibited are mattress or feather-bed turning or changing your sheets (you'll have bad dreams all week); egg gathering; sewing or knitting; and getting a haircut and manicure. It's a good day to put on your Sunday best (or at least clean clothes) and a nice day for a white wedding.

LUCKY NUMBERS

According to numerologists, two particularly lucky numbers are your Birthday Number and your Life Path Number (LPN). Your Birthday Number is considered your luckiest number, while your LPN represents who you are at birth and the traits you will carry with you through life.

Your Birthday Number is simply the day of the month you were born. So if your birthday is June 21, 1982, your Birthday Number is 21.

Calculate your LPN by adding up all the digits of your birth date and then adding the numbers as many times again as is necessary to reduce them to a single digit. So, again, if your birthday is June 21, 1982:

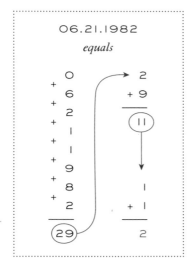

And all that numerology stuff aside, you may just have a number you really like or feel drawn to. And that's OK too. Whichever way you go, it's always good to have a lucky number (or three) handy whenever you need them . . . at the casino, when filling out that lottery ticket, or even when picking a hotel room for a night you want to get lucky.

MAKE A LUCKY DATE

Want to know if the date you're thinking about for your wedding is a lucky one? Or if you've picked the right day for that trip to Vegas?

One way to determine if a certain date is a lucky one is to calculate the Universal Day Number by adding up the numeric values of the month, day, and year until you're left with a single digit.

For example, if the date you want to check out is August 28, 2008...

First add all the numbers up like this:

MONTH + DAY + YEAR

08 + 28 + 2008 = (2044)

Then add the digits of that number together:

2 + 0 + 4 + 4 = (10)

Continue adding the digits as necessary until you arrive at a single digit:

1 + 0 = 1

So, the Universal Day Number for August 28, 2008 is 1.

If the Universal Day Number is a generally auspicious number or matches one of your personal lucky numbers, then go for it.

LUCKY DAYS AND COLORS

ARIES
March 20–April 19
Day: Tuesday
Colors: red and white

★

★   ★

VIRGO
August 23–September 22
Day: Wednesday
Colors: blue and gray

TAURUS
April 20–May 20
Day: Friday
Color: green

LEO
July 23–August 22
Day: Sunday
Colors: gold and orange

GEMINI
May 21–June 20
Day: Wednesday
Color: yellow

★   ★

★

CANCER
June 21–July 22
Day: Monday
Colors: silver and white

LIBRA

September 23–October 22

Day: Friday

Color: green

★

★

PISCES

February 19–March 19

Day: Thursday

Color: sea green

SCORPIO

October 23–November 21

Day: Tuesday

Colors: red and black

AQUARIUS

January 21–February 18

Day: Saturday

Colors: violet and sky blue

SAGITTARIUS

November 22–December 21

Day: Thursday

Color: purple

★

★

★

CAPRICORN

December 22–January 20

Day: Saturday

Colors: dark green and brown

PIMP MY LUCK

Many people have been aware of their birthstones and have even been receiving gifts that include them ever since, well, birth. Although it's true that your birthstone is lucky for you all year long, don't forget that it is particularly lucky during your birth month. Some people go the extra mile and buy all twelve stones, rotating them each month. If you're going to do this, be careful with the opal, since it is generally unlucky for someone not born in October.

There are several different lucky traditions working here, some ancient and some more recent. The modern list of birthstones was set in stone, as it were, during the twentieth century by a group of American jewelers. This standardized several traditional lists that had circulated for centuries, stemming from secular and nonsecular sources. For a little spice, there is also a mystical list that is associated with Tibetan astrology, and the Ayurvedic list that is associated with India's ancient medicinal practice.

And guys, don't think this section isn't for you. Although no one expects you to rush out and buy a ruby pinkie ring, there are plenty of other ways to incorporate a small stone into your wardrobe (think: cuff links, tie tacks, or dental bling).

LUCKY STONES

	MODERN	TRADITIONAL	MYSTICAL	AYURVEDIC
JAN	garnet	garnet	emerald	garnet
FEB	amethyst	amethyst	bloodstone	amethyst
MAR	aquamarine	bloodstone	jade	bloodstone
APR	diamond	diamond	opal	diamond
MAY	emerald	emerald	sapphire	agate
JUN	pearl moonstone	alexandrite	moonstone	pearl
JUL	ruby	ruby	ruby	ruby
AUG	peridot	sardonyx	diamond	sapphire
SEP	sapphire	sapphire	agate	moonstone
OCT	opal tourmaline	tourmaline	jasper	opal
NOV	yellow topaz citrine	citrine	pearl	topaz
DEC	topaz turquoise	zircon turquoise	black onyx	ruby

LUCKY MOLES

The Chinese believe that the location of moles on your face and body can reveal what sort of luck you will have, and they consult an almanac known as the Tung Shu *to find out the lucky (or unlucky) significance of their moles. In general, moles on the front of the body bring better luck, while the ones on the back tend to indicate bad luck or a burden to be carried. These diagrams pinpoint all the luckiest moles, so strip down and grab a mirror.*

BODY SPOTS

A Brings harmony and safety, and the smaller, the better.

B Indicates good luck with wealth, and if the mole touches your belly button . . . cha-ching!

C Brace yourself. This mole means you'll have good luck having children. Lots of them.

D Predicts lucky windfalls, especially if you have two.

E For men, a mole near the armpit means money, money, money. If it's deep inside the armpit, it also means prominent social status.

F Indicates inheritance luck for men; and for women, lucky wealth by their own efforts.

G Pack your bags, since good travel luck is coming your way.

H For women, this is a sign of luck in money.

ı Indicates success and wealth, especially in your own business ventures.

··

ɹ This mole suggests a rise to prominence is in your horizon.

··

ᴋ If found on the back of the thigh, it's a sign of good fortune.

MORE THAN JUST BEAUTY MARKS

A Good news: A mole here means you're lucky with money. Bad news: You're going to have to work for it.

B Indicates great family luck, with lots of children and grand-children; plus you'll be surrounded by love and support.

C In addition to being rich and famous, you'll be lucky enough to have a satisfying and balanced home life as well.

D Sweet talker, social mover and shaker, don't risk losing your luck by getting too full of yourself.

E Lucky in love, lucky in money. But don't let your weakness for good-looking strangers get you into trouble.

F Lucky for you a mole here means you'll never go hungry.

G Indicates authority and power are there for the taking.

H This mole indicates you will be vibrant into old age and you will be loved until the end. Is there any better luck than that?

I In order to enjoy the prosperity and recognition this mole says you have the luck for, you need to keep a lid on your excesses.

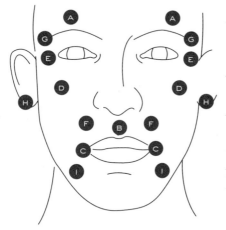

A SAILOR'S GUIDE TO TATTOOS

If you're looking to get a lucky tattoo, take some tips from sailors, who have figured out how to map good fortune directly onto the body.

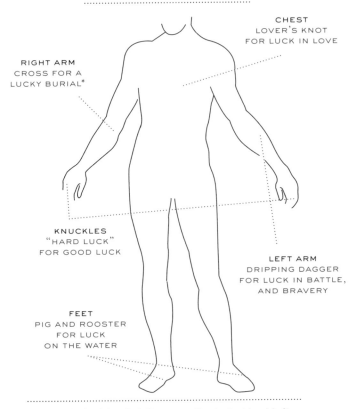

CHEST
LOVER'S KNOT
FOR LUCK IN LOVE

RIGHT ARM
CROSS FOR A
LUCKY BURIAL*

KNUCKLES
"HARD LUCK"
FOR GOOD LUCK

LEFT ARM
DRIPPING DAGGER
FOR LUCK IN BATTLE,
AND BRAVERY

FEET
PIG AND ROOSTER
FOR LUCK
ON THE WATER

Read: On land, in a Catholic country–if you're Jewish or Muslim, you may want to take a different route with this.

DIY LUCK

*What's behind the DIY (Do It Yourself) spirit is the desire
to take matters into your own hands and to create things
you want or need independent of paid professionals and
consumer culture. And just as you can redo your own kitchen
or publish your own zine, you can create your own luck.*

DIY CHARM

Carrying a charm is an effective way to attract good luck. Choose an object that feels lucky or one you just really like. Use your imagination (and a drill) to turn it into a necklace or a rearview mirror ornament, or laminate it and carry it in your bag. The important thing is that it serves as a reminder that good luck is there when you need it.

DIY RITUAL

Vaudeville comedians believed it was bad luck to crease their pants before performing, and so they had a ritual that required them to sit backstage in their boxer shorts before every show. Fine, maybe your lucky ritual won't involve old Jewish men kibitzing in their underwear, but it may involve a proscribed series of actions before every meeting or eating a certain food before every game. The important thing about a lucky ritual is that it makes you feel lucky and therefore receptive to good fortune.

LUCKY REMINDER

*Researchers who have studied lucky people have learned
that the single biggest predictor of the person who is lucky is
the person who feels lucky. And, if you haven't figured it out already,
we want that person to be you. Here is a place for you to write
down some lucky things about you. So when it feels like you can't
shake that bad-luck cloud, you can turn to this page to remind yourself that you can be—and, in fact, already are—that lucky person.*

LUCKY DAY

LUCKY NUMBER

LUCKY COLOR

LUCKY STONE

LUCKY BODY MARK

LUCKY CHARM

LUCKY RITUAL

BIBLIOGRAPHY

Bechtel, Stefan and Laurence Roy Stains. *The Good Luck Book.*
New York: Workman Publishing, 1997.

Brown, Simon G. *The Feng Shui Bible.* New York: Sterling, 2005.

DeLys, Claudia. *A Treasury of Superstitions.* New York:
Gramercy Books, 1997.

Gunther, Max. *The Luck Factor.* New York: Ballantine, 1978.

Hall, Judy. *The Astrology Bible.* New York: Sterling, 2005.

Opie, Iona and Moira Tatem. *A Dictionary of Superstitions.*
Oxford: Oxford University Press, 2005.

Pickering, David. *Cassell Dictionary of Superstitions.*
London: Cassell, 1995.

Potter, Carole. *Knock on Wood.* New York: Beaufort Books, Inc., 1983

Radford, E. and M.A. *The Encyclopedia of Superstitions.*
New York: Barnes & Noble Books, 1996.

Roud, Steve. *The Penguin Guide to the Superstitions of Britain
and Ireland.* London: Penguin Books Ltd, 2003.

Too, Lillian. *Total Feng Shui.* San Francisco: Chronicle, 2005.

Waring, Philippa. *A Dictionary of Omens and Superstitions.*
London: Souvenir Press, 1978.

Wiseman, Richard. *The Luck Factor.* New York: Hyperion, 2003.

ACKNOWLEDGMENTS

Our thanks go to:

Lara Harris, our designer, without whom this book would not have been possible; Mary Ellen O'Neill, Laura Dozier, Susan Kosko, Teresa Brady, Jean Marie Kelly, Felicia Sullivan, and everyone at Harper-Collins; Daniel Greenberg, Monika Verma, Elizabeth Fisher, and the folks at Levine Greenberg Literary Agency; Matthew Benjamin, Carrie Hornbeck, Kate Norment, Marina Padakis, John Siemssen, and Cynthia Smedstad.

The following people, who provided assistance in our research: Andrea Balboni, Kate Blumm, Marcelo Cardoso, Michael de Zayas, Matthias Ernstberger, Mark Fisher and everyone at the Brooklyn Botanical Gardens, Michael Fromm, Christina Gallagher, Nicole Haghighi and Pär Gustafsson, Esther Hang McKinley, Angela Izrailova, Marilynn Gelfman Karp, Michael Korda, Brankica Kovrlija, Elizabeth Kwan, Ellen Kwan, Sophia Lambrakis, Alicia Lubowski-Jahn, Bonnie Maslin, Erin McDermid, Glenn Mott, Alexis Rodriguez-Duarte and Tico Torres, Steven Rubin, Stefan Sagmeister, David Sangalli, Steve Shay, and Rosemary Yeap.

Our family and friends, who gave us suggestions, advice, and support. We're lucky to have you.*

....

*Hokey, but true.

THE SOCIETY FOR
FORTUITOUS EVENTS

The Society for Fortuitous Events is devoted to the documentation, classification, and preservation of luck. From the conservation of lucky beliefs, traditions, and practices around the globe, to the compilation of individual good luck stories, the Society's mission is to promote and disseminate the knowledge of all things lucky. Please visit www.societyforfortuitousevents.com.

Deborah Aaronson and Kevin Kwan are Trustees of the Society for Fortuitous Events. Aaronson is a writer and editor who lives in Brooklyn and Kwan is a writer and photographer who lives in Manhattan. They are both wearing red underwear right now.

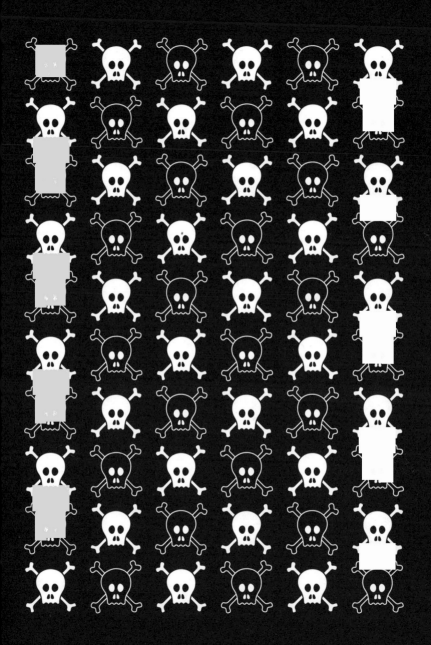

BLACK CAT

WHY IT IS UNLUCKY

A Norse legend tells of the goddess Freya, who rode in a chariot pulled by black cats. When the Norse converted to Christianity, Freya was recast as a witch, and it was said that after seven years of service, she rewarded the cats by turning them into witches (masquerading as black cats). In the Middle Ages, it was believed that if a black cat crossed your path it was a) a sign that a witch was around, b) a witch in disguise, or c) an indication that the devil was taking notice of you. Whichever the case, none boded well, and it is still believed today that black cats should be avoided. Some say that if black cats are left to their own devices, they will perch by the bedside of babies and the elderly to suck the breath out of them.

THE FLIP SIDE

In ancient Egypt, the goddess Isis considered all cats sacred, and her daughter, the goddess Bast, was represented by a black cat. In Japan black cats are considered lucky, as they are in England, particularly if they walk into your house uninvited. Even some American folklore suggests that if a strange one comes to your door it will bring you good luck. Many sailors believe that a black cat on board will ensure a safe passage, and many sailors' wives adopt black cats to guarantee their husbands' return.

ANTIDOTE

Spitting after you see a black cat will stop any bad luck in its tracks.

BREAD

WHY IT IS UNLUCKY

Was Atkins ever right when he made us all scared to eat bread. Not only is it loaded with carbohydrates and calories, but it's a veritable minefield of bad luck. It is a sign of bad luck if a loaf of bread splits while baking. It's bad luck to burn bread (it's said to be food for the devil). An air pocket discovered in a loaf of bread is thought to be the sign of a grave and an omen of death. An overturned loaf of bread is also a predictor of death, and a piece of buttered bread dropped butter-side down is bad luck, as well as bad breakfast. It's bad luck to cut off the top of a loaf of bread, to cut it from both ends as opposed to cutting from one end, or to take the last piece unless it's offered to you. And never leave a knife stuck in a loaf of bread—that's bad luck, too.

THE FLIP SIDE

Bread plays a significant role in many religious traditions and ceremonies. Bread given to a newborn ensures it will never go hungry, and bread brought into every room in a new home guarantees a never-empty pantry. A loaf of bread dropped on the floor is thought to be a good omen; make a wish while you're picking it up and your wish will come true. Whoever is offered and eats the last slice of bread will have luck with love or lots of money.

ANTIDOTE

There's not much you can do if you have a bad bread incident, so just try to avoid the ones you can as much as possible.

BREAKAGE

WHY IT IS UNLUCKY

It may feel like someone's kicking you when you're down to hear that breaking something is unlucky. And it may feel like someone's kicking you when you're down and walking off with your girlfriend to hear that breaking something is likely only the preamble to two more breakages. The general rule of thumb is that bad things come in threes—and breakage is no exception. It's considered especially unlucky to break a shoelace, something that was given to you as a love token, or a wedding ring. A mirror is probably the worst thing you can break, and seven years of bad luck are said to follow. It's unclear why such heavy penalties are placed on something that's already distressing, but sources suggest it's related to a symbolic connection to death or separation.

THE FLIP SIDE

On special occasions, Greeks are known to break plates as an expression of *kefi*, or "joy."

ANTIDOTE

The best thing to do after you've broken something is to simply identify two other things that you don't really care about and break them before you accidentally break two other things you do care about. You can also try breaking the thing that you just broke two more times. The gods of luck don't seem to differentiate between "by accident" and "on purpose" in this situation; they just want more broken stuff.

BROKEN MIRROR

WHY IT IS UNLUCKY

Although breakable mirrors didn't make an appearance until four-teenth-century Venice and weren't readily available in England until the late seventeenth century, man could always see his reflection in shiny surfaces, including lakes and ponds. And he believed that what he was looking at was not just his image reflected, but also his immortal soul. As a consequence, any disturbance of the image was believed to cause injury. Although over time mirrors became more common-place, and man a bit more enlightened, the nagging suspicion that a broken reflection was bad news persisted. The common belief is that if you break a mirror, seven years of bad luck will follow, although other superstitions abound. You shouldn't let a baby look into a mirror for its first year, or it will come to harm. You should cover all the mirrors in your house after another resident has died, so that his soul won't get caught in the mirrors and be detained. And if a mirror falls off the wall, it means a death in the family.

THE FLIP SIDE

There is pretty much no flip side to this.

ANTIDOTE

If you break a mirror, wash the pieces in a south-running river. If you can't find a river, let alone one that is south running, pound the broken mirror into pieces so fine that no one could ever see themselves in it again. If you can't do this, just bury the pieces.

BROOM

WHY IT IS UNLUCKY

We all hate housework, but who knew it could be so dangerous? As the vehicle of choice for witches, brooms are loaded with negative connotations, and unlucky beliefs related to them are plentiful. You should never take an old broom along when moving into a new home, nor should you give your old one away, lend it, or burn it—that's all bad luck. If you come across one lying on the floor, do not step over it. Related to the rules governing brooms are prohibitions related to sweeping. Never sweep out your front door—you'll be brushing away your good fortune—and it's also bad luck to sweep the dirt from one room to the next. Sweeping should also never be done after dark. And someone sweeping over your feet is no good for your love life.

THE FLIP SIDE

A new broom is the perfect housewarming gift (although one should never be purchased in May). Laying one across an entranceway can protect you from unwanted visitors. And throwing a broom after someone embarking on a business venture or fishing trip is said to bring good luck.

ANTIDOTE

Although it seems contrary to common sense, always brush dust into the house rather than out to retain good luck. Be sure when you're finished with your broom that you set it bristle-end up, and don't leave it in a corner.

CANDLE

WHY IT IS UNLUCKY

It's no real surprise that one of the main occupations of people sitting around in dark homes lit only by candlelight was thinking about candles. As a result, unlucky candle beliefs abound. It's bad luck to light more than two candles off of the same light or to have three candles burning in the same room. Candles should never be lit using the fire from a fireplace. Various patterns made by melting wax that are too complex and dull to explain in detail were said to be an omen of death, and a blue flame meant the presence of a spirit and possibly an imminent death. It's bad luck to leave a candle burning, and this includes one left in an empty room as well as one on your birthday cake.

THE FLIP SIDE

Candles play an essential role in many traditions, and have long been thought to keep evil spirits at bay. The one exception to the No Candle Left Behind law is on Christmas Eve and New Year's Eve, when it's considered good luck to keep a candle burning even after you go to bed. Candles can be pricked with a pin to force a negligent loved one to pay more attention to you. A candle blown out accidentally is said to be an indication of an upcoming marriage, and a sparking wick is the sign of the arrival of a stranger or a letter.

ANTIDOTE

There is little you can do once you've made a flame-related faux pas, so do your best to avoid them.

*Although dropping something isn't in itself bad luck
(unless, of course, it breaks), there are prohibitions against
picking up certain things after you have dropped them.
The following is a list of things that are better left where they are.*

COMB	HANDKERCHIEF	SCISSORS
CUTLERY*	NEEDLE	SOAP***
GLOVE	RING**	UMBRELLA

ANTIDOTE

Having someone else pick it up for you is the simplest
solution, but keep in mind it's bad luck to thank the person
for doing so. If no one else is around, stepping on the
object before picking it up should help reverse the bad vibe.

**Also a good predictor that a visitor will soon appear. Knife = man;
fork = woman; spoon = child. **Particularly bad luck at a wedding, during the
ceremony. ***Although we're not sure what to recommend if you're in the shower
since all but the very lucky shower alone and stepping on soap seems hazardous.*

EVIL  EYE

WHY IT IS UNLUCKY

According to many cultures around the world, some people (and even some animals or inanimate objects) are in possession of what is known as the "evil eye," or *malocchio*, as it is called in Italy. That is, the ability, with one look, to cast misfortune. Those particularly suspected of having it include: people with different colored eyes; folks with deep-set, close-set, or crossed eyes; black cats; and peacock feathers. And those given to speaking compliments are thought to be likely targets.

THE FLIP SIDE

When the name of something starts with the word *evil*, it's fair to assume it's pretty much all bad.

ANTIDOTE

Arm yourself with a good-luck charm, including a *Nazar Boncugu* (Turkish evil-eye beads), a *Hamsa* or *Hamesh* hand, or an Egyptian Eye of Horus. Wearing mascara or lining your eyes with kohl is an easy (and attractive) way to protect against the evil eye. If someone gives you the evil eye, spit in their eye three times or outstare them, which doesn't require as good aim. For long distance evil-eye prevention, make the *mano cornuto* (stick out your little finger and your index finger while folding down your thumb and other fingers) or the *mano fico* (curl your fingers down and put your thumb between your middle and index fingers). If a situation is ripe for a compliment, say the Yiddish *"Keynehore"* ("May no evil eye harm you") after you've spoken.

"GOOD LUCK!"

WHY IT IS UNLUCKY

There are few things that are guaranteed more likely to bring some-one bad luck than to wish them "good luck!" It is deemed all the more damning if said to an actor, a sailor, or a gambler. Lucky laws maintain that drawing attention to a desire before it happens (for example, that someone should succeed, have a safe trip, or win money) is simply tempting fate; it is the one sure way to make evil spirits jealous and motivate them to see that the good thing doesn't happen.

THE FLIP SIDE

If you've wished someone "good luck," and are looking for a possible upside, there is none. Go directly to the antidote.

ANTIDOTE

Of course, there are many things that you can say instead of "good luck!" Even the most amateurish thespian knows to say "break a leg" instead of "good luck" to a fellow actor, or, you can take a page from the French, who believe stepping in dog poo is good luck, and say "merde!" to a dancer before a show. The general rule seems to be this: the worse the outcome you indicate, the better the result. And, if you have made the mistake of wishing someone "good luck," you can immediately reverse the effects by knocking on wood.

GREEN

WHY IT IS UNLUCKY

As a famous frog once said, it's not easy being green. And it turns out that it's not lucky either. Although the color green has many positive associations, with nature and youth, for example, it is the unluckiest of all the colors. Some suggest that green is unlucky because it was the favorite color of fairies and wood spirits and wearing it would lay a person open to their influence. However, there is little evidence that these creatures had a special liking for green, let alone that they even existed at all (which is another story entirely). Green is thought to be an especially unlucky color choice for costumes in the theater, for brides, or for lovers, who are known, on occasion and with certain provocations, to turn into green-eyed monsters. Some even say that if you wear green, you'll soon be wearing black.

THE FLIP SIDE

Well, they seem to feel differently about this in Ireland, where green is the national color. And there are many instances where green is a positive: you give the "green light" to something you want to go ahead; skills in the garden reflect a "green thumb"; and to move on to "greener pastures" is to move on to something better.

ANTIDOTE

There is no known cure, so it's best to avoid it as much as you can.

HATS

WHY THEY ARE UNLUCKY

Hats are tricky things and must be handled with care in order to prevent disastrous results. Mistakenly putting a hat on backward is a bad omen, and hats should never be worn inside a home. Perhaps the most serious consequences accompany the setting of a hat on a bed, which invites extreme misfortune and likely death. Some suggest the reason behind this is the perceived defilement of the sacred nature of the bed (the site of many crucial activities, including conception, birth, and death). Others suggest it is related to the lost hope of a visiting doctor who, in rushing to see his bedridden patient, forgets to remove his hat until he realizes that there is nothing left to be done, and then simply tosses it onto the bed in resignation. Neither explanation is altogether satisfying, but the belief nonetheless persists.

THE FLIP SIDE

Intentionally turning a hat around back to front or inside out is a tried-and-true way to reverse bad luck.

ANTIDOTE

If you make the mistake of putting on your hat backward, the only solution is to go out and buy a new one. Spitting inside a hat is a known way of outing the bad stuff, and having to do so might make you think twice before dropping it on a bed again.

MAGPIE

WHY IT IS UNLUCKY

The sight of a single magpie is a known harbinger of bad fortune, particularly when you're setting off on a trip. A group of them heard chirping away is likely hatching some sort of evil plan. A much-repeated rhyme (with many variations) suggests that the future can be told based on their numbers: "One for sorrow, two for mirth, three for a wedding, four for a birth, five for silver, six for gold, seven for a story never to be told." Not necessarily bad, but spooky, right? The earliest *magpie = no good* references appear in the twelfth century, although some say the bird earned its bad reputation by refusing to wear full mourning (its feathers are black and white) at the Crucifixion.

THE FLIP SIDE

Despite its bad rap in the West, in China the magpie is known as the "bird of fortune" or "bird of joy" and it is thought to bring both luck and good news.

ANTIDOTE

Magpies should not be harmed for fear of making matters worse. To avert bad luck, if you see a magpie you can say, "Good morning, Mr. Magpie," spit, or, if you're wearing a hat, tip it to the bird. You can make the sign of the cross (spectacles, testicles, wallet, and watch) and if you're not wearing a hat (or testicles for that matter), say, "Magpie, magpie, chatter and flee. Turn up thy tail, and good luck fall me."

POINTING

WHY IT IS UNLUCKY

Although we often find ourselves doing so without even thinking about it, pointing is not only bad manners, but it's bad luck. This includes pointing at people as well as pointing at objects. Witches were considered master pointers and able to cast spells simply by pointing at their victims, and even mere mortals are considered able to direct bad luck by pointing. Even though we've all found ourselves pointing out Orion's Belt or the Big Dipper while lecturing to a bored companion (or being lectured to), it is considered highly unlucky to point at the sun, the moon, the stars, or even at a rainbow. So it seems the celestial gods like being pointed at just about as much as any of us do. Ships at sea are acutely susceptible to the effects of pointing; drawing attention to something so vulnerable is simply tempting fate.

THE FLIP SIDE

There is no flip side. Pointing is to be avoided.

ANTIDOTE

If you find you absolutely must point at something, do so with your entire hand rather than with just one finger. Apparently the gods who oversee pointing regulations get confused when a whole hand is waggled rather than a single finger, and you may squeak by. But if you do forget and point by mistake, spit on the offending finger right away to reverse the bad luck.

WHY IT IS UNLUCKY

Unlike now, for centuries salt was a scarce, expensive, and therefore precious commodity, and superstitions around its use and abuse have been around for a long time. Anxieties surround both the lending and borrowing of salt (don't do it) and also the act of passing salt to someone at the dinner table ("Help me to salt, help me to sorrow"). Yet most well known are the dangers accompanying spilling salt. Some say that each fallen grain represents a tear that will later be shed. More practical would be the explanation that since salt was so dear, wasting it through careless spilling was to be avoided. What better way to stigmatize the act than with larger-than-life consequences?

THE FLIP SIDE

Known to both preserve and improve the taste of food, salt can be lucky as well. It can be burned as a protective measure against ill wishers or thrown at someone who just delivered a curse. Salt is an auspicious gift to bring to a newborn or as part of the New Year's Eve ritual and is a useful good-luck charm to bring with you when moving into a new house. It can also be flung after a person who has visited your home who you don't wish to return.

ANTIDOTE

If you happen to spill some salt, grab a pinch with your right hand and toss it over your left shoulder (into the eyes of the devil who is, probably unbeknownst to you, perched there).

STAGE FRIGHT

*Actors are among the most superstitious people around and,
as a result, there's a whole host of things to avoid when working in
showbiz. Here are a few of the top things to steer clear of.*

....

PEACOCKS

Stay away from them, their feathers, and even fabrics
or wallpapers that have peacock-inspired designs.

"MACBETH"

Shhhhhhh! Don't ever say that name anywhere
near a theater! If you must refer to this Shakespearean
tragedy, call it "the Scottish play."

WHISTLING

Don't ever whistle—not during rehearsals, not in a
dressing room, or, basically, not anywhere inside a theater.

"GOOD LUCK!"

Even the most theatrically impaired probably know
better than to say this to a person about to go onstage.
Preferable is "break a leg," which does not call attention to
the unseemly and possibly desperate desire for fortune.

ANYTHING REAL
Antiques, jewels, food, flowers, money, mirrors, and Bibles.
Often accused of being phonies themselves, actors are much better
off if they use ersatz replacements instead of the real thing.

UMBRELLAS
Opening an umbrella onstage is to be avoided. If you must
because of stage directions, be sure to use the always
effective antidote of opening the umbrella pointing to the
ground as opposed to over your head or in midair.

CATS
Although cats are generally thought to be good luck in theaters,
letting one cross the stage is deemed to have disastrous results.

LIGHTS
Failure to leave a light always burning in the theater can be
an invitation to ghosts to take up residence; they may make their
presence known in the form of tricks, mishaps, and pranks.

PEEKING
Never look out at the audience from the side of a dropped curtain.

GREEN
Avoid wearing any green clothing onstage.

KNITTING
Although it probably wasn't the first thing you planned
to do in the wings, avoid knitting there at all costs.

REHEARSALS
A good one can only mean a bad performance.
It is also unlucky to speak the final lines of a play during
rehearsal or, in fact, anytime before opening night.

RIGHT FOOT
Always be sure to exit the dressing room left foot first
(yes, we know the header says "right foot," we mean that
figuratively, not literally). And don't worry if you
stumble up to the stage, because even though stumbling
is bad luck in most other contexts, it's good luck here.

MAKEUP
It's bad luck to spill the contents of a makeup box or to
clean it up if you've done so. It's also unlucky to apply makeup
standing behind someone while looking into their mirror.

STAIRS

WHY THEY ARE UNLUCKY

Who knew the humdrum act of going up or down the stairs is actually laden with unlucky possibilities? It is considered unlucky if two people pass each other on a staircase; if you stumble while going down the stairs; if you go up or down the stairs partway and then turn around. Dating back to the nineteenth century, the fear of stairs is likely rooted in the possibility that meeting a stranger on a dark, narrow, and often poorly lit staircase would leave you vulnerable to attack.

THE FLIP SIDE

Although stumbling *down* the stairs is bad luck, stumbling *up* the stairs can mean good fortune, and possibly a wedding in the future.

ANTIDOTE

Simplest is to wait at the head or foot of the stairs for the other person to ascend or descend before taking to them. If the passing is unavoidable, you should both keep your fingers crossed as you pass to avoid bad luck. Alternatively, say something (anything) to the other person while passing. If you've started out on the stairs and realize you must go back, continue all the way in the direction you were going, rest a moment when you reach your original destination, and then turn back. This solution will seem perfectly reasonable at home, and much less appealing if you're halfway up the Washington Monument. If you do happen to stumble up the stairs, and welcome the opportunity to get married, don't look back after doing so.

STARS

WHY THEY ARE UNLUCKY

Although many of us have heard the expression "Count your lucky stars," when having escaped a dreaded outcome by a hair's breadth, stars haven't always been so lucky. Dating back to the seventeenth century, the sight of a falling or shooting star was said to foretell death or disaster. Count them if you will, just don't point at them (even when not counting), as it is considered insulting to the celestial gods and may lead to sudden death (either yours or someone else's).

THE FLIP SIDE

Many people (chiefly followers of astrology) think that they have a lucky star guiding their destiny, and many cultures believe stars can determine fate. Interestingly, the Hebrew words *mazl tov*, which are generally translated as "good luck," are more accurately translated as "good constellation," a wish that the stars be well aligned. Jiminy Cricket (and many others before and after him) believed that stars could be wished upon. This includes shooting stars and the first star of the evening sky. If you're looking for cold, hard cash, say, "Money, money, money" to a shooting star before it disappears. When wishing on a first star: "Star light, star bright, the first star I see tonight, I wish I may, I wish I might, have the wish I wish tonight."

ANTIDOTE

Pointing at a star with an entire hand instead of a finger is a way to avoid bad luck; if you forget to do so, spit on the offending finger.

STEPPING ON A CRACK

WHY IT IS UNLUCKY

This unlucky event harkens back to an old childhood chant, which appears in various forms both in the United States and the United Kingdom. In case you've only ever heard the "crack" part, here's one version in its entirety: "Step in a hole, you'll break your mother's sugar bowl. Step on a crack, you'll break your mother's back. Step in a ditch, your mother's nose will itch. Step on the dirt, you'll tear your father's shirt. Step on a nail, you'll put your father in jail." The crack is thought to represent the opening of a grave, and to walk on a grave was considered hugely unlucky. That doesn't really explain what a hole has to do with a sugar bowl, but who really has the energy to parse this whole thing? Clearly this saying was invented and perpetuated by people who didn't have to walk on sidewalks made of crack-prone cement, where it's practically impossible not to do damage to your poor mother.

THE FLIP SIDE

Unfortunately, it's impossible to put a positive spin on crack stepping.

ANTIDOTE

No known antidote exists; just do the best you can to avoid cracks.

STUMBLING

WHY IT IS UNUCKY

Given all of the precautions generally taken at the start of something new to ensure continued success, it's no surprise that to begin a journey, a new day, or a venture with a stumble is thought to be a bad sign of the road ahead. Stumbling on the way to the altar does not bode well for a marriage, and tripping at a gravesite is a notable bad omen. A stumbling horse is unlucky too. Thresholds have major symbolic import, and stumbling when crossing one is particularly inauspicious. A decidedly spooky explanation behind these beliefs suggests that the human soul is a fragile thing, likely to get jostled out of one's body during a clumsy episode. More to the point, perhaps, is the simple belief that a stumble, although not a disaster in itself, is the outward sign of one to come.

THE FLIP SIDE

Although stumbling when going *down* the stairs is bad luck, stumbling when going *up* the stairs is actually thought to be a sign of good luck, and may even be the sign of an imminent wedding.

ANTIDOTE

The best way to counteract clumsy footwork is to follow the time-honored tradition of spinning around in place three times. This evidently is like a lucky "reset" button and allows you to start all over again as if the unlucky thing never happened in the first place.

TABLE MANNERS

Although your mother may have warned you against putting your elbows on the table, she may not have known there are a whole host of things that are much worse to rest there. Seen as altars of the domestic environment, tables should be treated with reverence, and there are not only things that should never be placed on them, but also things that should never be done over—or passed over—them.

Placing a bellows on a table is sure to cause a fight.

....

It's bad luck to place a baby or a saucepan on a table.

....

A broom or dustpan should never be placed on a table or passed over a table, and a broom never used to sweep a tabletop.

....

It's inauspicious if a cat leaps over your table.

....

Don't pass a chair over a table; it's bad luck.

Knives should never be laid across one another on a table.

....

Lanterns are unlucky to place on a table—particularly for farmers ("A lantern on the table, a death in the stable").

....

Never shake hands over a table.

....

Shoes and umbrellas should never be placed on a table.

....

Never sit on a table. If an unmarried woman does, she may never get married. If two people do, it means they will argue.

TEMPTING FATE

WHY IT IS UNLUCKY

One of the themes running through many lucky (and unlucky) traditions is the belief that reveling in good fortune, through words or actions, is likely to draw the attention of evil spirits. Being evil spirits, once they hear about something good, they want nothing more than to take it away—often with disastrous results. It is therefore ill-advised to speak directly of something good or to act on a happy event before it has come to pass. It is considered especially hazardous to bring a crib into a home before a baby has been safely born, to wish an actor "good luck" before he or she begins a performance, to hang a calendar before the turn of the new year, to sing before breakfast (you'll "cry before night"), or to admit to being either healthy or happy when asked. You might think that having to avoid all things positive will leave you feeling somewhat bereft, but just think of the fun you'll have telling your brother how ugly his new girlfriend is.

THE FLIP SIDE

Nope. No flip side.

ANTIDOTE

The list of things one shouldn't do for fear of tempting fate is daunting. But don't fear. There are a number of ways to cut bad luck off at the pass if you've done something to tempt fate. Try knocking on wood, saying the Yiddish "*Keynehore*" (roughly translated as "no evil eye"), or spitting immediately after the offense has been committed.

THIRTEEN

WHY IT IS UNLUCKY

The fear of the number thirteen (triskaidekaphobia) seems to have gotten kicked off by the ancient Hindis, who believed having thirteen people seated together was unlucky. The first unlucky thirteenth guest we know by name was the Norse god Loki, who showed up to a dinner party uninvited and had another guest killed. Perhaps the most infamous seating of thirteen was the Last Supper, with Judas Iscariot the unwelcome guest. A more general fear of the number thirteen has become so pervasive that today many tall buildings skip the thirteenth floor; hotels often don't have a room numbered thirteen; and thirteen loaves of bread are called a "baker's dozen" to obviate the need for anyone to have to actually say the number aloud. Friday the thirteenth is considered a singularly unlucky day, and it remains unlucky to have thirteen to dinner, since it is believed one of the thirteen diners will die within a year of the event.

THE FLIP SIDE

Among the Chinese and the Egyptians, the number thirteen is regarded as lucky (they have their own thoughts about which numbers are unluckiest).

ANTIDOTE

If you find yourself at a table with twelve others, you should all join hands and stand as one. This should prevent the imminent death of any of the diners.

III

THREE

WHY IT IS UNLUCKY

An old saying goes, "Bad things come in threes." One death is thought to be followed by two more; if you break something, two additional breaks will occur; and, in fact, it is believed that any sort of accident you have will naturally lead to two others. Lighting three cigarettes off a match is thought to carry the same penalty. In one story, with many variations and set during different wars, three soldiers are sharing one match at night. The duration of the light allows the third smoker to be spotted and killed by enemy fire. So, if smoking doesn't kill you . . .

THE FLIP SIDE

Another saying goes, "The third time's the charm," the sentiment of which dates back to the fourteenth century. Many legends involve the granting of three wishes, three chances, or revolve around spells that need an action repeated three times to work. Odd numbers generally have more positive connotations than even ones, and three has a long-standing place in mystic and religious traditions (think Holy Trinity). It is said to be lucky to sneeze three times in a row, and many of us (including those who grew up on Sesame Street or listened to De La Soul) believe three is a magic number.

ANTIDOTE

Artificially finish off the unlucky threesome before fate steps in. If you break something, break two other things you don't care about.

TURNING BACK

WHY IT IS UNLUCKY

The belief that it's bad luck to turn back to retrieve something you've forgotten once you have begun a journey dates back to the Middle Ages. Fishermen and miners on their way to work, as well as people leaving for other significant events, such as a wedding, feared it above all others. Although some point to Lot's wife as the earliest example of this superstition, others correctly argue that a) she hadn't actually forgotten anything and b) she hadn't tried to return; she merely turned back to look. A more likely explanation relates the belief to the notion that something begun well will end well; turning back is seen as a journey started poorly, which would, logically, end poorly.

THE FLIP SIDE

There isn't really any upside to turning back and you should avoid doing so whenever possible.

ANTIDOTE

The best thing to do is to try to fool evil spirits into thinking that your journey was actually completed and that you're now going home, only to set off on an entirely different trip a few minutes later. So, say you want to go shopping but you've forgotten your wallet, which you realize in the middle of your driveway. Sit down in the driveway as if that was where you were planning to go all along and then get up and go inside. When inside sit for a moment, grab your wallet, and then depart for your "new" destination (the store).

UMBRELLA

WHY IT IS UNLUCKY

The belief that opening an umbrella indoors will bring bad luck likely has its roots in the most practical of reasons. The umbrellas used at the time this belief first appeared, in the late nineteenth century, were operated with a stiff spring, which was difficult to master and potentially painful if mishandled. If an umbrella was opened indoors, the likelihood of it knocking into some Victorian knickknack greatly increased. The Victorians were also, apparently, scared for their furniture finish, bedspreads, and toes, as it was similarly considered unlucky to place an umbrella on a table or on a bed or to drop one.

THE FLIP SIDE

Early examples of umbrellas are found in the eleventh century BC in China, Egypt, and Babylon. In Japan they were used as emblems of state, and for the Hindus even today they symbolize great power as one of the Eight Glorious Emblems of India. Protectors not only from the sun and rain, umbrellas, it was believed, could also shield important personages from malevolent spirits. The Chinese believe a closed umbrella situated inside a home, near the entrance, will protect it.

ANTIDOTE

If you've mistakenly opened an umbrella indoors, close it quickly and spin around in place (umbrella in hand) three times. If you're forced to open one on a theatrical stage, where the superstition is also found, point it toward the floor rather than overhead while opening it.

WALKING UNDER A LADDER

WHY IT IS UNLUCKY

Walking underneath a ladder when it is leaning against a wall is sure to bring misfortune. A leaning ladder forms a triangle with the ground, and breaking this triangle by walking through it is thought to be a violation of a universal symbol of life. Some also say that each side of the triangle represents one part of the basic family unit (mother, father, child), and passing through it is a violation of the sanctity of the family.

THE FLIP SIDE

Ladders have long been seen as symbols of good luck. The Egyptians placed them in tombs to help the souls of the dead climb to heaven, and, while alive, carried charms in the form of ladders to help them avoid earthly temptations and ascend to greater spiritual heights.

ANTIDOTE

Good thing there are a number of ways to reverse the effects of this unlucky event, should it occur. Quickly make a wish while still under the ladder. Cross your fingers until you see a dog, or cross your fingers and spit three times through the rungs on the ladder. Spit on your shoe and leave it to dry. Walk backward through the ladder to the point where you started your walk.

WHISTLING

WHY IT IS UNLUCKY

Although it's totally fine to whistle while you work if you're a podiatrist, if you're a journalist in a newsroom it shouldn't be done. The same goes if you are a miner (it's thought to cause disasters underground), a sailor (it's known to raise storms at sea), or an actor (and it's even worse if you're in a dressing room). It's also considered bad luck to whistle after dark or to whistle inside a home. All of these prohibitions are related to the fear that whistling draws unwanted attention from evil spirits or is seen as an invitation to the devil to join you. It was long believed that women should not whistle. An old proverb (with some variations) goes, "A whistling woman and a crowing hen are neither fit for God nor men." Although neither phenomenon is that unusual, both were seen as females displaying "male" traits, and therefore as unnatural and prohibited. An added inducement for girls not to whistle was the belief that it would cause them to grow beards.

THE FLIP SIDE

As long as you're not in a newsroom, a mine, a theater, or a home; at sea; or a woman, whistle away.

ANTIDOTE

The cure for whistling in any unwanted circumstance is to circle the place where the offense occurred three times. Or good electrolysis.

WHITE

WHY IT IS UNLUCKY

Newly engaged women may be distressed to learn that many things that are white are considered to be unlucky. The list of white creatures it is bad luck to cross paths with includes: cats, cows, rabbits or hares, horses, and birds. White flowers (lilies, lilacs, and snowdrops, among others) are unlucky to bring indoors and, because of their association with funerals, are not recommended as gifts for someone who is sick unless you really want to do them in for good. Although fairy tales and westerns always have the good guys riding to the rescue on white horses, they were thought to foretell danger and sometimes murder.

THE FLIP SIDE

White is thought to be the color of innocence, a protective and holy color, and is an excellent choice for clothes on many important occasions, including weddings. White nightclothes are believed to protect the sleeper from evil spirits. In many Asian countries white is a symbol of both purity and happiness, and is the color worn for mourning, as seeing a loved one pass into a better life is a moment for celebration. And although many associate the white elephant with a burdensome possession, it is considered sacred in many countries in the Far East.

ANTIDOTE

When coming across any of these unlucky white creatures, spitting—either at the creature itself or over your left shoulder—is an effective antidote. Just remember, there's no need to spit at the bride.

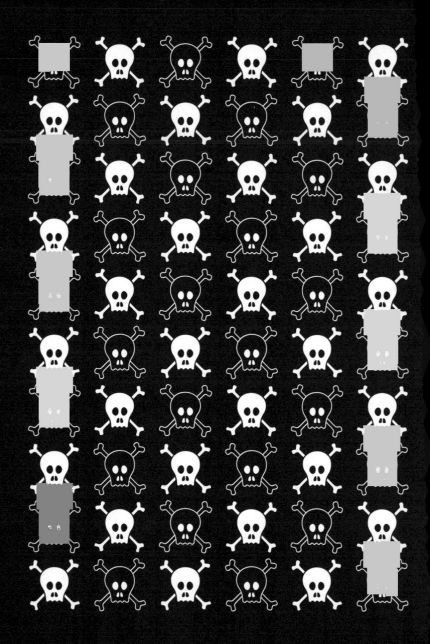